34.10

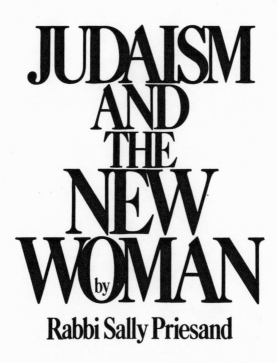

JUDAISM AND THE NEW WOMAN

by

Rabbi Sally Priesand

Introduction by **BESS MYERSON**

BEHRMAN HOUSE, INC. NEW YORK

THE JEWISH CONCEPTS
AND ISSUES SERIES

Series Editor: SEYMOUR ROSSEL

246.387
P949j
1975

Art Motif: Bronze sestertius, issued 71 C.E., Mint of Rome
depicts Titus (?) in armor standing at left holding short
sword symbolic of victory. At right a weeping captive
Jewess symbolizes Judaea. Legend reads: IVDAEA CAPTA
("Captive Judaea").

Design by Marsha Picker

For my mother

...וְתוֹרַת חֶסֶד עַל לְשׁוֹנָהּ

Proverbs 31:26

ACKNOWLEDGMENTS

The editor and publisher thank the following for permission to reprint:
Bruno Bettelheim for selection from his article "Portnoy Psychoanalyzed"
© 1969 by *Midstream*. Zena Smith Blau for selection from her article "In
Defense of the Jewish Mother" © 1967 by *Midstream*. Central Conference
of American Rabbis for selection from "Report of Committee on Ordination of
Women" in *CCAR Yearbook* Volume 66 © 1956 by Central Conference of
American Rabbis. Central Conference of American Rabbis for selection from
"Responsum on Question, 'Shall Women be Ordained Rabbis?'" by Jacob Z.
Lauterbach in *CCAR Yearbook* Volume 32 © 1922 by Central Conference of
American Rabbis. *Council Woman* for selection from "Not For Men Only"
by Sally Priesand © 1974 by *Council Woman*. Ezrat Nashim for selection from
statement distributed at Rabbinical Assembly Convention © 1972 by Ezrat
Nashim. Hadassah for selection from *Women in Israel* by Molly Lyons
Bar-David © 1952 by Hadassah. Harvard University Press for selection from
Marriage Laws in the Bible and the Talmud by Louis M. Epstein © 1942
by Harvard University Press. Except reprinted by permission of Hawthorn
Books, Inc. from *Shalom, Golda* by Terry Morris © 1971 by Terry Morris.
All rights reserved. Herzl Press for selection from *Women Build a Land*
by Ada Maimon © 1962 by Herzl Press. Ichud Habonim Labor Zionist
Youth for selection from "Israeli Women Need Liberation" by Shulamit Aloni
in *Sisters of Exile: Sources on the Jewish Woman* © 1973 by Ichud Habonim
Labor Zionist Youth. International Universities Press, Inc., for selection from
Life is With People by Mark Zborowski and Elizabeth Herzog published by
Schocken Books Inc., © 1962 by International Universities Press, Inc. *The
Jewish Digest* for selection from "Old Disease in New Form: Diagnosing
Portnoy's Complaint" by Arthur J. Lelyveld © 1969 by *The Jewish Digest*.
Keeping Posted for selection from "From Promise to Reality" by Sally
Priesand © 1972 by Union of American Hebrew Congregations. Jacob R.
Marcus for selection from his article "The First Woman Rabbi" © 1972 by
The American Israelite. Excerpt reprinted by permission of Julian Messner,
A Division of Simon & Schuster, Inc., from *Eloquent Crusader: Ernestine
Rose* by Yuri Suhl © 1970 by Yuri Suhl. National Council of Jewish Women
for selection from *The First Fifty Years* © 1944 by National Council of Jewish
Women. G. P. Putnam's Sons for selection from *A Land of Our Own* by
Golda Meir, edited by Marie Syrkin © 1973 by G. P. Putnam's Sons. *Response*
for selection from "The Changing Role of Women in the Jewish Community"
by Jacqueline K. Levine © 1973 by *Response*. Excerpt reprinted by permission
of Schocken Books Inc. from *Hannah Senesh Her Life and Diary* by Hannah
Senesh © 1966 by Hakibbutz Hameuchad Publishing House Ltd., English
edition © 1971 by Nigel Marsh. Seven Arts Feature Syndicate for selection
from "The Woman Rabbi" by Martha Neumark in *The Jewish Tribune* © 1925
by Seven Arts Feature Syndicate. Marie Syrkin for selection from her article
"The Fun of Self-Abuse" © 1969 by *Midstream*. Union of American Hebrew
Congregations for selection from *The Lifetime of a Jew* by Hayyim Schauss
© 1950 by Union of American Hebrew Congregations. Excerpt reprinted by
permission of The Viking Press, Inc., from *Henrietta Szold: Life and Letters*
by Marvin Lowenthal © 1942 by Marvin Lowenthal, © renewed 1970 by
Herman C. Emer, Harry L. Shapiro, Executors for the Estate of Marvin
Lowenthal. Walker & Company, Inc. for selection from the book *The Story
of Anna O.* by Lucy Freeman published by Walker & Company, Inc. New
York, N.Y. © 1972 by Lucy Freeman. *Women's World* for selection from
June issue © 1974 by *Women's World*. World Union for Progressive Judaism
for selection from *The Growth of Reform Judaism* by W. Gunther Plaut
© 1965 by World Union for Progressive Judaism. World Union for Progressive Judaism for selection from *The Rise of Reform Judaism* by W. Gunther
Plaut © 1963 by World Union for Progressive Judaism. Herman Wouk for
selection from *Marjorie Morningstar* published by Doubleday & Company, Inc.,
© 1955 by Herman Wouk.

CONTENTS

3 JEWISH WOMEN IN THE MODERN WORLD

4 CREATING TOMORROW'S JEWISH WOMAN

INTRODUCTION

> "If women have always held an honored and respected position in the Jewish tradition, why does Jewish law so obviously discriminate against them?"

That is the inescapable question which Sally Priesand asks and analyzes in JUDAISM AND THE NEW WOMAN. It is a question as new as the new woman, but it is also a question as ancient as Judaism itself.

Jewish women asked it of Moses almost before he had a chance to sit down and rest after carrying the tablets from Mount Sinai. As a result of their protests, elements of *Halachah* (Jewish law) were changed by Moses himself.

In the countless generations since then, many more changes have been made, but some basic discriminations survived, and the need to ask the question has remained a part of our religious experience, just as the questioning of other discriminations has remained a part of the human experience for all women, in every land, in every religion.

"Separate but equal" is the traditional rationale in religious law as well as civic law, but that can be as opportunistically evasive of truth and justice in organized religion as it is in any other facet of social challenge.

Sally Priesand is a unique person of great faith and scholarship. She is the first woman to be ordained by any theological seminary into the rights and privileges of the rabbinate. Both her life and her book are deeply rooted in the Jewish tradition, in the human richness of her religious and cultural heritage, but she lives and writes with a universal understanding of the assigned roles of men and women in organized religion and organized society (and the way each role may help to shape and dictate the other), and she gives eloquent voice to all women everywhere, of any religious or cultural heritage, who resist an imposed status of second-class citizen or second-class worshipper. Men may also profit from what she has to say—except, of course, those with a terminal case of hard of hearing.

Even self-evident truths need a receptive climate in which to survive and flourish. It is significant that Rabbi Priesand's book is published during International Women's Year, when many "traditions" are being measured and tested, to separate those which are healthy and all-encompassing from those which are merely inequities hallowed by age. In 1895, the social climate was not receptive for equal rights pioneer Elizabeth Cady Stanton when she published *The Woman's Bible,* her views on the double standard in her own and all organized religions. The result was a public uproar—man–made, Mrs. Stanton charged—that frightened even the suffrage movement into disowning the book at its convention. "Only" 80 years later, Rabbi Priesand's book is not only accepted as a profound work of scholarship, but it is being issued by a long-established publisher of religious books as a text for use in the formal curriculum of both religious and secular schools. In that respect, it is a milestone in social progress: before there can ever be a change of ideas, there must certainly be a free exchange of ideas. We cannot learn from each other if we do not listen to each other.

JUDAISM AND THE NEW WOMAN is one perceptive woman's view of the rules of Jewish life and worship that are arbitrarily limiting to the full expression of women's abilities and aspirations. It examines those rules that are considered *halachic* and therefore legally binding, rules that are rooted in a past when women were considered transferable property—from fathers to husbands and even, after they were widowed, to the families of their husbands. It also examines the extra-legal customs that continue even today, undermining right and defying reason, circumscribing the participation of women in their communities, in their homes, in the practice of their faith.

Her sources range the history of her people, from the Bible and the Talmud to contemporary literature, and she has found in the texts and between the lines the true story of women suppressed and women emerging. What she has given us is an adventure story of human effort, as she shares with us her own search for the freedoms that can only strengthen faith.

The thoughts she will stir in her readers are as traditional as the Bible and as topical as the Equal Rights Amendment. She asks and answers questions that are myth-slayers. Among them:

Why did Adam leave Lilith for Eve?

Were the wives of the Patriarchs the original Jewish Mothers?

Would you do what Esther did?

Why did Vashti refuse to do what Esther did?

Must feminism and faith be mutually exclusive?

With scholarship, and with the attention-holding skill of a storyteller who has a good story to tell, Rabbi Sally Priesand has added an important, pioneering volume to the library of liberation, raising the consciousness of Jewish women and all women to many of the deepest reasons we are what we are, and do what we must do, in the greatest of human efforts: the quest for true identity, beyond distortion, beyond myth, beyond all artificial obstacles. JUDAISM AND THE NEW WOMAN is a firm, assured step forward in that quest.

BESS MYERSON

PREFACE

On June 3, 1972 I was ordained rabbi by Hebrew Union College-Jewish Institute of Religion in Cincinnati, Ohio. As I sat in the historic Plum Street Temple, waiting to accept the ancient rite of *s'micha* (ordination), I couldn't help but reflect on the implications of what was about to happen. For thousands of years women in Judaism had been second-class citizens. They were not permitted to own property. They could not serve as witnesses. They did not have the right to initiate divorce proceedings. They were not counted in the *minyan*. Even in Reform Judaism, they were not permitted to participate fully in the life of the synagogue. With my ordination all that was going to change; one more barrier was about to be broken.

When I entered HUC-JIR, I did not think very much about being a pioneer. I knew only that I wanted to be a rabbi. With the encouragement and support of my parents, I was ready to spend eight years of my life studying for a profession that no woman had yet entered. My decision was an affirmation of my belief in God, in the worth of each individual, and in Judaism as a way of life. It was a tangible action declaring my commitment to the preservation and renewal of our tradition.

As one would expect, there were problems even as I worked toward ordination. Though Reform Judaism had long before declared an official religious equality between men and women, Reform Jews still believed that a woman's place was in the home. They no longer insisted that men and women sit separately during worship services. They allowed women to be counted in the *minyan*, to conduct the service, to serve as witnesses in ritual matters. They demanded that girls receive a religious education equivalent to that provided for boys. They allowed women to become members of the congregation with the privilege of voting and they even permitted them to be elected to offices on synagogue boards. But they were not yet ready for the spiritual leadership of a woman.

Undoubtedly, many believed that I was studying at HUC-JIR to become a *rebbetzin* rather than a rabbi, to marry rather than to officiate. Four years passed (while I concentrated on my studies at the University of Cincinnati) before people began to realize that I was serious about entering the rabbinate. During that time, I felt that I had to do better than my classmates so that my academic ability would not be questioned. Professors were fair, but occasionally I sensed that some of them would not be overly upset if I failed. And when, in my fifth year, I was ready to serve my first congregation as student rabbi, some congregations refused to accept my services. Still the members of Sinai Temple in Champaign, Illinois, received me warmly.

My sixth year of study brought the beginning of a tremendous amount of publicity. When you are a "first," you are expected to be an expert in everything. Personal appearances, interviews, statements on contemporary issues —all are expected. Surprisingly enough, though I have always considered myself an introvert, I somehow managed to cope with these new pressures. It helped to know that by this time I had the support, or at least the respect, of most of the members of the college community. Dr. Nelson Glueck, the late president of HUC-JIR, was a particular source of strength. His courage in accepting me as a rabbinic student made possible my eventual ordination.

As my eighth and final year drew to a close, I was faced with finding a job. Some congregations refused to interview me. I was disappointed and somewhat discouraged by these refusals. But since I had not expected everyone to welcome me with open arms, I had prepared myself for this possibility. I knew that I needed only one acceptance and I never really doubted that I would find one synagogue ready to accept me.

The offer of a position as assistant rabbi at the Stephen Wise Free Synagogue in New York City was a blessing in the true sense of the word. I have been extremely well-received by the members of the congregation, and it has been my privilege to work with and to learn from Rabbi Edward E. Klein, the senior rabbi. My activities have not been limited to one area of the Synagogue. My duties include conducting worship services, preaching on Shabbat, teaching both in the Adult Institute and in the Religious School, supervising the youth program, advising a biweekly study group, lecturing to the Golden Age Club, counseling, officiating at life-cycle events, and attending all committee meetings. The only area in which people have shown any real hesitancy has been that of my officiating at funerals.

In addition to my congregational responsibilities, I have lectured extensively throughout the country—an activity which has shown me that congregations and rabbis are ready for change. Ten years ago, women were much more opposed to the idea of a woman rabbi than were men. Since then, however, the feminist movement has made a tremendous contribution in terms of consciousness-raising, and women now demand complete and full participation in synagogue life. This is a significant development because changes will not be made until we change the attitudes of people.

Men and women must learn to overcome their own psychological and emotional objections and regard every human being as a real person with talents and skills and with the option of fulfilling his or her creative potential in any way he or she finds meaningful. Women can aid this process—not by arguing but by doing and becoming, for accomplishments bring respect and respect leads to acceptance. Women must now take the initiative. They should seek and willingly accept new positions of authority in synagogue life.

It is still too soon to assess the impact of my ordination, but I would hope that it would at least mark a transition in our congregations, that sole involvement on the part of women in the synogogue kitchen and the classroom should move toward complete and full participation on the pulpit and in the boardroom as well.

When I accepted ordination on June 3, 1972, I affirmed my belief in Judaism and publicly committed myself to the survival of Jewish tradition. I did so knowing that Judaism had traditionally discriminated against women; that it had not always been sensitive to the problems of total equality. I know that there has been a tremendous flexibility in our tradition—it enabled our survival. Therefore, I chose to work for change through constructive criticism. The principles and ideals for which our ancestors have lived and died are much too important to be cast aside. Instead we must accept the responsibilities of the covenant upon ourselves, learn as much as possible of our heritage, and make the necessary changes which will grant women total equality within the Jewish community.

That is the purpose of this work, then: to examine Jewish tradition in terms of its view towards women, to struggle with our own identity as Jews in the modern world, and to suggest ways in which we can adapt Judaism to allow women full and complete participation in the life of our people.

1
HISTORICAL
ASPECTS

CHAPTER ONE

The Biblical Concept of Womanhood

If women have always held an honored and respected position in Jewish tradition, why does *Halachah* (Jewish law) so obviously discriminate against them? Why has it taken so long for women to function as rabbis and cantors? Or even in other leadership roles within the Jewish community? How can we provide new role models for Jewish children? What changes can we make within organized religion to encourage women to participate? These, and many others, are issues of concern. To deal with them, we must understand how we got where we are today.

BIBLICAL WOMEN

The Bible begins with the story of creation. Two different versions are given of the creation of woman. In Genesis 1, man and woman are created equal. In Genesis 2, woman is created out of man's rib. This contradiction led to the development in Jewish legend of the Lilith myth. Much of the legend is folklore, but the Jewish elements are easily seen. The most popular form of the myth is as follows:

> When God created Adam, He also created a wife for him out of the earth. This first woman was Lilith. Adam

and Lilith, however, did not make a happy couple. Because they were both of the same origin, she considered herself his equal and refused to obey him. They quarreled with one another until in a moment of rage, with the help of the ineffable name of God which she uttered, she flew away from Adam and vanished into the air.

Adam complained to God that the wife He had given him had deserted him. God sent three angels to bring her back. The angels found her in the Red Sea, in the very spot the Jews later passed in the Exodus from Egypt. The angels tried to make her return, threatening that if she would not, hundreds of her demon children would die daily. Lilith preferred this punishment to returning to Adam.

Again the angels threatened: they would drown her in the sea. She implored them to spare her, and in return she granted them a concession. She told them that her purpose in life was injuring babies. Until the eighth day, after their birth, she could injure boys; and girls until the twentieth day. But, she swore, whenever she would see the names of these three angels written in a home, she would keep away from child and mother, and would do no injury.

The three angels released Lilith after she had taken that oath. And to this day, the names of these three angels are written on amulets and hung upon the walls of the room where a woman lies in childbed.[1]

The legend reflects an early Jewish position on the equality of women. Lilith was punished for her independence. Her desire was to be Adam's equal, but this did not coincide with the scheme of things. From the very beginning, according to this legend, women were expected to "mind their manners" and "hold their tongues." It was Eve, over whom God commanded Adam to rule, who would find a place in official Jewish history.

POINT OF VIEW

The Lilith myth serves a double purpose. First, it tells us something about the society in which it was written. Second, and more important, it sets standards of behavior.[2] For thousands of years, women have been taught that it is dangerous to be like Lilith. Independence, aggression, self-assertion, and strength are not admirable qualities for women to possess. It is better to be submissive like Eve. As a result, women have suppressed their own desires and obeyed the wishes of their husbands. While men have been leaders, rabbis, scholars, and authorities, women have for the most part been unassuming and modest, living vicariously through the men in their lives. Even today, most girls are taught to be wives and mothers. Isn't it about time that we present Lilith as an acceptable role model, that we encourage our daughters to be bold and daring?

And what of other women in the Bible? The matriarchs, Sarah, Rebecca, Rachel, and Leah, are honored and respected by Jewish tradition. They are portrayed as over-protective mothers concerned with the preservation of a people. As instruments through which that people would survive, they did anything and everything that was required of them—even if that sometimes meant acting in ways unworthy of praise.

Sarah's envy led to the banishment of Hagar and Ishmael. Rebecca's love for Jacob led to his acquisition of the birthright and his journey to Haran in search of a wife. Rachel's theft of Laban's idols eventually led to his treaty with Jacob. The matriarchs were guilty of jealousy, favoritism, and robbery, but they acted to protect Israel. They perceived the immediate dangers that threatened Israel's destiny and pushed their sometimes blind husbands into action. They were devoted and decisive.

But above all else they were mothers, and that fact would be impressed upon the mind of every Jewish girl whose father blessed her on *Shabbat* with the traditional words, "May you be like Sarah, Rebecca, Rachel, and Leah." For whatever else this blessing may have meant, it most certainly expressed the wish that the young woman would marry and have children—and not be at all like Lilith.

There are some bright spots in the biblical treatment of women, but they are few and far between. Miriam was a prophetess, Deborah a judge, Huldah a woman of learning. Ruth's devotion to Naomi was unmatched. Her loyalty and her conversion to Judaism inspired the rabbis to view her as the great-grandmother of King David. Esther saved her people from the cruel Haman, but she was able to approach the king only because he loved her. On the other hand, we hear little of Vashti, who refused to be treated like an object. Her open defiance of the king's command to appear before his guests that he might show her off with his other possessions was ample reason for punishment. She was too much like Lilith.[3]

The ideal woman, as described in Proverbs 31:10–31, rises early and works late. She spins and weaves and labors in the field. She provides for her family and cares for the poor. She supervises the household so that her husband will have time to sit in the gates among the elders of the land. She is praised for her strength and dignity.

Scholars tell us these words are an example of the high esteem in which women have always been held. They are customarily recited by Jewish husbands each *Shabbat,* and it is improbable that many Jewish women are laid to rest without having this passage recited at their funeral. Nonetheless, the first verse is bothersome. "A woman of valor who can find? For her price is far above rubies." It is as if the writer were saying: "These are the qualities of the ideal woman, but unfortunately she is nowhere to be found."

FAMILY STRUCTURE

The ideal woman was a wife and mother. In biblical times family organization was of the type called patronymic. Marriage represented ownership, and the husband owned his wife just as he owned his slaves.[4] The wife was purchased by the groom's family, and payment of the purchase price, or *mohar,* reimbursed the bride's father for the property loss he sustained when she got married. In other words, marriage was a business transaction, the groom's family gaining someone who would tend the flock, draw water from the well, and assist with household tasks and the bride's father losing valuable property and a useful member of the family.

For all practical purposes, a girl had nothing to say about the choice of her future husband. Her father arranged the match, and although she may have been consulted (Gen. 24), it was not until after the negotiations had been completed. She had little choice but to accede to that which her entire family had already agreed.

While a man was clearly the master of the house (Gen. 3:16), children were commanded to give their mother the same respect due their father (Ex. 20:12, Lev. 19:3, Ex 21:17). This was probably the only area in which there was a certain equality between husband and wife. It suggests to us that a woman must have been treated with respect by her husband; otherwise, could she have sustained the respect of her children?

A CHANGE IN ATTITUDE

While the biblical woman was always subject to male domination, a new moral attitude toward women began to develop. For example, in Exodus 21:1–11, only the male servant was freed after six years of service. The later deuteronomic code, however, commanded that the female servant should also be set free (Deut. 15:12–17).

A major difference can also be seen in the two versions of the Ten Commandments. In Exodus 20, the last of the commandments reads: "Thou shalt not covet thy neighbor's house . . . thy neighbor's wife, nor his man-servant, nor his maid-servant, nor his ox, nor his ass, nor anything that is thy neighbor's." The neighbor's house was his most precious possession, and it was mentioned first. In Deuteronomy 5, the order has been changed and the prohibition against coveting your neighbor's wife comes first. She was no longer quite on the same plane as a man's other possessions; she was beginning to be regarded as a real human being.

POINT OF VIEW

It is often pointed out in an apologetic way that the status of the biblical woman in Jewish tradition was not as low as that of women in other cultures. For example, Hebrew morality was clearly superior with regard to prostitution. Israelite women were never exposed to the vicious practices of other nations, many of which encouraged prostitution as a form of religious worship. Time and again, the people of Israel were commanded not to imitate the sexual immorality of other nations. Jewish fathers were forbidden to turn their daughters into prostitutes (Lev. 19:29), and the daughters of Israel were forbidden to become prostitutes (Deut. 23:18).

That Hebrew women were the most exalted of ancient women, however, does not excuse the secondary position assigned to them. The biblical concept of womanhood influenced generations to come and is in large measure responsible for the inequality that still exists today. It is deeply rooted in the human psyche, and change must be resolved before significant advances can be made. The legal views expressed in the Bible reflect a society much different from our own, and they must be reinterpreted in every generation to maintain their relevance.

SOTAH

Another example of the double standard in biblical times concerns adultery. When a woman was suspected of being unfaithful, she was forced to undergo an unbelievably disgusting and dehumanizing ordeal, in which she was cursed by a priest and then made to drink water into which he had put "the dust that is on the floor of the tabernacle" (Num. 5:11–31). This ritual, referred to as *sotah,* was based on the premise that if the woman were innocent she would suffer no ill effects. But if she were guilty, her guilt would be obvious through the physical effects she would suffer. One wonders, however, whether any woman, or for that matter any man, could go through such a humiliating experience without becoming physically ill and actually dying.

POINT OF VIEW

It is significant that no punishment was provided for the man who was involved in the act of adultery. The fact is that according to Jewish law, a man could not be guilty of adultery with respect to his own wife because he had no legal obligation to be faithful to her.[5] Only a woman, because she was the property of her husband, could commit adultery. A man was permitted to have as many wives as he wished. Once again women were singled out and humiliated in the eyes of the community. Shouldn't God's seventh commandment apply equally to men and women?

ॐ

LEVIRATE MARRIAGE

This view of women as property may also be seen in the case of levirate marriage and its laws. When a woman's husband died, she became the property of the collective family. The head of the family controlled her, just as he had control over all family possessions. All valuable and productive property was meant to be used, and since the widow was still capable, she was no exception.

These circumstances led to the custom of levirate marriage. A member of the deceased's family was required to marry the widow. Thus, the family's property right in the widow was preserved. In the case of a childless marriage, a second motive became apparent: to ensure that the deceased would have a child to bear his name and become his heir. This did not require marriage, merely intercourse between the widow and a member of her husband's family. The child born of such a union was considered a child of the deceased husband, and in this way the deceased was assured of descendants. A third motive was added as primitive life developed—to protect the community. Insisting upon levirate marriage meant that the widow would not become a burden on the community. She would be cared for, sheltered, and sustained by her husband's relatives.

From the time of her husband's death until the occurrence of the levirate marriage, a woman remained in the state of *zikah*. This rabbinic term means "being chained," and a woman could be released from *zikah* in only two ways: through the acceptance of levirate marriage or through the ceremony of *halitsah,* in which the obligation of levirate marriage is refused.

In deuteronomic times (seventh century BCE) it was considered disgraceful for a man to refuse to marry his widowed sister-in-law (Deut. 25:5–10). By postexilic times (fourth century BCE), however, the ceremony of *halitsah* was considered the proper thing for the brother-in-law to do in order to free the widow and make it possible for her to marry the man of her choice (Ruth 4).

The option of performing the *halitsah* ceremony is given first to the oldest brother. If he refuses, then the option falls to the other brothers in order of age. If all refuse, then the oldest brother must either marry the widow or perform *halitsah.* In all this, the widow has no choice. Even if she prefers to remain single for the rest of her life, she is forced to undergo *halitsah* in order to release her brothers-in-law from their obligation.

Halitsah is described in the Bible as a public ceremony; therefore, a full court is necessary. The proceedings are as follows:

> The judges sit and the *levir* (the brother-in-law) and widow stand before them. The court ascertains that they are of age and that three months have passed since the husband's death. Witnesses are called to testify to the identity of the *levir* and the widow. The *levir* is asked whether he consents to the *halitsah* rite, and on his affirmative answer, he is placed in position for the removal of his shoe. That is, he leans against the wall or against an indoor post. The ceremonial shoe is of a special kind, made all of leather, even to the seams and strings. The *levir*'s right foot is washed before the ceremonial shoe is put on; the shoe is then donned, laced up, and tied below the knee. When thus ready, he presses his foot on the floor.
>
> The woman, facing the *levir* and prompted by the head of the court, audibly recites in Hebrew the biblical

phrase: "My husband's brother refuseth to raise up unto his brother a name in Israel; he will not perform the levirate duty unto me."

The *levir* also replies audibly in Hebrew, reciting after the head of the court the biblical phrase: "I do not wish to take her."

Then the woman, bending down, loosens the strings of the shoe with her right hand; thereafter, holding up his foot with her left hand, she pulls off the shoe with her right hand and throws it on the ground. She straightens up and spits upon the ground before the *levir*'s face in sight of the court, and exclaims in Hebrew (as prompted again by the head of the court): "So shall it be done to the man that doth not build up his brother's house, and his name shall be called in Israel, the house of him that had his shoe loosed." Those present at the ceremony all exclaim together in Hebrew, *Haluts hana'al!* (he that hath his shoe loosed) three times.[6]

While the ceremony of *halitsah* is observed by some Jews even today, the Reform rabbinate unanimously passed a resolution in 1869, stating that "the precept of levirate marriage, and eventually of *halitsah,* has lost to us all meaning, import and binding force."

A resolution to the same effect was passed by the Jewish Synod held at Augsberg in 1871. It reads as follows:

The Biblical precept concerning the *halitsah* has lost its importance, since the circumstances which occasioned the levirate marriage and the *halitsah* no longer exist, and the idea underlying the whole precept has become foreign to our religious and social views.

The nonperformance of the *halitsah* is no impediment to the widow's remarriage.[7]

The concept of levirate marriage developed as an attempt to preserve the family's property right in the widow, to ensure the presence of a child to inherit the deceased man's name and share of the estate, and to protect the community. The widow had no choice in the matter; she was forced to do as the family pleased. If her brother-in-law wished to marry her, she was compelled to marry him even if she preferred to remain alone for the rest of her life or to marry someone else. If he did not wish to marry her, she was obligated to participate in the *halitsah* ceremony. Either way, freedom of choice was out of the question. Woman as an individual capable of making those decisions affecting her personally was ignored and her position as a human being degraded.

POINT OF VIEW

The laws of levirate marriage and *halitsah* are a disgrace to the dignity of woman. That they are still adhered to today is even more shocking. Orthodox rabbis who say that legal equality for Jewish women is impossible merely ignore the fact that Jewish law has never been static. There are numerous examples of reinterpretation in other areas of tradition. Why must the fate of childless widows remain totally in the hands of possibly spiteful brothers-in-law?

CHAPTER TWO

Rabbinic Attitudes Toward Women

MARRIAGE

In rabbinic times, marriage was a business transaction. As in all business ventures, a contract had to be signed. This contract is called a *ketubah,* and has been described as a "legal document embodying the essential points agreed upon by the parties and sanctioned by the law as to the manner of their living together as husband and as wife." [1]

The rabbis provided for the contract to include a series of clauses. The first was called the marriage clause. It contained the formula which concluded the marriage. The original marriage declaration was: "She is my wife and I am her husband from this day and forever." It was later changed to: "Be thou my wife according to the law of Moses and Israel."

The second clause included a promise to pay the *mohar* and the *mattan.* The *mohar,* or purchase price, represented the essence of the *ketubah.* A virgin was worth 200 *zuzim* and a nonvirgin 100 *zuzim.* The *mohar* was paid by the groom to the bride's father for his daughter's hand. As years passed, however, important changes took place in the institution of the *mohar.* The father of the bride held the money in trust for his daughter, and eventually it was no longer paid but promised. In this way the groom was permitted to use it in his business on the condition that he guarantee payment of it by all the property he possessed.

Mattan refers to the voluntary gift that the groom gave the bride. It was given in addition to the *mohar* and was recorded separately. Its amount depended upon the social standing of the couple. As with the *mohar,* the *mattan* was originally given in cash and only later became a promised sum to be paid in the event of divorce.

The amount of the dowry was stipulated in the third clause. It represented a daughter's share of her father's estate. The sons inherited the family fortune while the daughters received dowries as a substitute. The dowry belonged to the daughter; it was her private possession. In later times the dowry became a parental obligation meant to attract suitors. It was a wedding gift to the groom under terms of tenancy. Tenancy meant that the groom could use it for his needs. He could not sell it, however, because title to it remained with his wife.

As a result of constant pressure, the husband's tenancy rights were eventually transformed into practical ownership. By the second century the husband, not the wife, was clearly the owner of the dowry. In the event of divorce, however, the wife could demand its return.

At first there was no standard amount for the dowry and fathers gave what they could. Later a dowry of 50 *zuzim* was made compulsory. An orphan received the money from her father's estate and a girl whose father was too poor to pay the minimum dowry received the money from charity funds.

The fourth clause concerned succession. Biblical law establishes the order of succession as follows: son, daughter, father. Mother and wife inherit nothing. Through a series of legal changes, rabbinic law granted the husband priority in matters of succession first over the father, then over the daughter, and finally over the son. The Jewish court retained the power to modify this order.

The conditions for divorce were included in the fifth clause. A woman could not divorce her husband, but she could institute divorce proceedings, asking the court to force her husband to grant her a bill of divorce. The husband, on the other hand, had full freedom to divorce his wife without cause. If she committed adultery or if she burned his food or if she simply found no favor in his eyes, he could send her away. One of the main purposes of the *ketubah,* however, was to discourage divorce, for the *ketubah* came to represent the divorce price for which the husband was responsible. It meant that he had to pay the *mohar* and the *mattan,* forfeiting all gifts that he had given to her. It also meant the return of the dowry in a sum equal to its value at the time of the marriage. These conditions tended to discourage divorce.

Clause six discussed mistreatment and expulsion. It later became a statute of law, however, because it had to provide for various kinds of mistreatment that simply could not be listed in the *ketubah.*

Polygamy was the subject of the seventh clause. While both biblical and rabbinic law permit polygamy, it is not encouraged. In the tenth century Rabbi Gershom enacted a prohibition against it. (This applied only to European and not to Oriental Jews.) Before this time, however, the wife usually demanded the insertion of a clause in the *ketubah* obligating her husband to take no other wife.

POINT OF VIEW

History tells us that polygamy was not encouraged. In fact, it was seldom authorized by the rabbis except in cases where a man's first wife remained childless for ten years.

In order to produce an heir, a man was permitted to take a second wife. The law permitting polygamy, although rarely used, remains intact for Oriental Jews.

Judaism did respect a woman's right to sexual fulfillment, but the second-class status of women is quite evident with regard to sexual attitudes. That polygamy was an acceptable life-style is another example of how laws were made by men for men. Male sexual freedom was upheld throughout ancient Hebrew culture. Women were expected to be faithful to one man (even if they had to share him with others), while their husbands could add variety to their sexual lives. The only prerequisite was proof that they could support another wife. Undoubtedly, polygamy was practiced with the hope that male children would be added to the clan. Daughters were acceptable but one truly rejoiced over the birth of sons.

The eighth clause of the *ketubah* contained a promise to give the wife food, clothing, medicine, ransom, burial, and marital satisfaction. A husband was required to provide for his wife according to his means and according to the standard to which she was accustomed. The rabbis stipulated the minimum amount of food that was to be given to the wife, as well as the appropriate garments and household articles. Proper medical service was promised to her in case of illness, and the rabbis declared that it was morally wrong for a man to divorce a wife while she was sick even if she was chronically ill and her illness was causing his economic ruin.

The ransom clause is one of the oldest in the *ketubah*. It requires the husband to redeem his wife should she be taken captive under such circumstances as piracy, highway robbery, bedouin attacks, or warfare. Such occurrences were not infrequent in rabbinic times and on into the Middle Ages.

The husband's obligation to provide burial for his

wife was rarely expressed in the *ketubah*. The rabbis did not like to mention such a gloomy subject as death at the time of the couple's joy. The obligation was clearly recognized, however, and even the poorest husband had to provide a grave and funeral procession for his wife.

A further basic obligation of Jewish marriage is sexual intercourse between husband and wife. It became the husband's duty to see that this obligation was fulfilled. According to rabbis, the frequency of intercourse depended upon the husband's vocation. For example, a laborer could be absent from his wife for a week, while a student was permitted to be away for a month. Failure to fulfill the sexual obligation was sufficient grounds for divorce.

Here again, we see the heavy hand of the pro-male prejudice. A man was fined for his "rebellion" in not fulfilling his sexual obligations. A woman was also fined, but her penalty was higher. Eventually the following procedure developed:

> For a period of four weeks, announcement in the synagogue is made on every Sabbath of her rebellion against her husband, and at the end of that period a court messenger warns her that if she does not yield she will be divorced and forfeit her *ketubah*. If she persists, she is given a year's separation from her husband without support, and thereafter she is divorced with the total loss of her *ketubah,* taking with her of her dowry only what she can get possession of. The *gaonim* of the seventh century modified the procedure, out of fear that the woman might institute proceedings in a Gentile court. They did away with the year's separation, and ordered her to be divorced immediately with the forfeiture of her *mohar* and *mattan*.[2]

This may have increased synagogue attendance among town gossips, but it certainly showed little sensitivity for a woman's feelings.

The rabbis provided for a ninth clause, to include a promise from the husband to pay his wife's debts. But no *ketubah* containing such a clause has been found. Jewish law states that the husband is not responsible for any debts his wife incurred prior to their marriage. Neither must he pay her debts incurred after their marriage unless she was forced to borrow money because he failed to support her.

The tenth clause contains an order providing for the support of the widow and any young daughters out of the estate after the husband's death. This ensured the widow's right to a dwelling and maintenance, and in normal circumstances the widow continued to live as she had when her husband was alive. Since daughters did not share the inheritance of their father's estate, provisions were also made for them until they came of age (twelve years and one day). In biblical times a woman always belonged to some master, whether it was her father or her husband or her children. In rabbinic times, however, she was completely independent when she came of age. Therefore, her father had to provide for her only until that time, although he also had to set aside a specific marriage portion, which she received at the time of her wedding.

The eleventh clause developed in an effort to provide sufficient security for the wife. The *ketubah* was considered a loan, with the wife as creditor and the husband as debtor. The lien clause protected the wife, for it stipulated that all the husband's property would serve as security for the *ketubah*. It was payable upon divorce or upon the husband's death.

Other provisions meant to protect the wife were made in special clauses added to the *ketubah*. For example, the husband might promise never to sell anything that belongs to his wife without her consent and never to force her to move to another city without her approval. The *ketubah* may also contain a clause that provides for a conditional divorce to be granted the wife in the event that her husband falls seriously ill. The divorce would become effective a moment before the husband's death and would enable the wife to avoid the whole matter of *halitsah*.

In summary, the *ketubah*, or marriage contract, listed the agreements made by husband and wife as they entered upon marriage. The major thrust of the document was to protect the wife, grant her security, and ensure that she would be provided for in the event of divorce or death. The development of the document shows a significant change in the attitude toward women, a change which for the most part, displayed concern and sensitivity for women as human beings. There are still Jews who write a *ketubah* at the time of marriage, but the modern *ketubah* contains a minimum of clauses and is written mainly to perpetuate an ancient tradition.

POINT OF VIEW

The traditional *ketubah* is meaningless today. The bride and groom do not accept it as a real document and have no intention of following its stipulations—even if they understand what it says. Mention of the 200 *zuzim,* for example, is irrelevant and serves only to perpetuate the view of marriage as a business transaction in which the groom purchases his bride.

Although the *ketubah* itself is pointless, the concept behind it may still have meaning for us. If couples were to write a modern marriage contract, they would have to search out their stand on various issues. They would be forced to determine the values on which to base their new life together. They would have to discuss beliefs and differences, conflicts and problems. Drawing up the *ketubah* could be a means of confronting one another. It might well prevent problems in later years.

DIVORCE

Only men possessed the power of divorce. Divorce originally meant driving out of the house. Since the man
owned the house, he had the right to drive his wife out of
it. The wife could not drive him out because she did not
own it. A bill of divorce was also intended to free one
to marry another. Only a woman needed to be freed to
marry again, since a man could have as many wives as he
wanted; therefore, only a woman could be divorced.

While the power of divorce lies with the husband
alone, several changes were made to protect the welfare
of women. As we have already noted, the *ketubah* developed in such a way as to make it difficult for a man to obtain a divorce. In addition, the rabbis decreed that a woman
has a right to demand a divorce under circumstances such
as the husband's refusal to support her, his marital in-
fidelity, or his cruel treatment of her. In these cases, the
Beit Din (rabbinic court) was obligated to compel the
husband to divorce her. The rabbis also possessed the
right to annul any marriage whether directly or retroactively, and Rabbenu Gershom (eleventh century) decreed
excommunication for the husband who divorced his wife
against her will.

The divorce proceedings were as follows: The husband and wife appeared before the rabbi in the presence of
two witnesses, one scribe, and a *Beit Din* made up of three
rabbis. The scribe brought the necessary utensils for the
writing of the *get* (bill of divorce), and the husband purchased them because the *get* had to be written on paper
owned by the husband. The scribe wrote from one to a
hundred slightly differing divorce documents until the
Beit Din accepted one of them. Both the husband and the
wife were asked if they agreed to the divorce without
compulsion. All vows and promises which would make the

get invalid were annulled. The two witnesses signed the *get* and then the husband gave it to the wife. He did this by folding it and dropping it into his wife's hands. The wife gave it to the *Beit Din* and they read it to make certain that it was correct. The document was then cut with a knife and deposited with the rabbi, who kept it permanently. The husband and wife received a note from the rabbi attesting to the divorce.

POINT OF VIEW

Although the rabbis discouraged divorce and exhibited a definite concern for the fair treatment of wives, Jewish divorce laws obviously discriminate against women. A wife is condemned to remain with her husband no matter how unbearable or dissatisfying she finds their marriage. A husband, on the other hand, needs no greater reason to divorce his wife than her failure to please him.

These laws, based on the belief that a woman is a husband's possession, remain in force today. They are humiliating and degrading, and place a woman at her husband's mercy. Modern rabbinic authorities must realize that discouraging divorce is not enough. A woman cannot maintain her dignity and self-respect unless she is accepted as an equal partner in marriage. This requires a change in the law and an outright rejection of principles which are crude and primitive by modern standards.

Changes made it more and more difficult for a husband to obtain a divorce. Still Jews did not revert to some of the common practices that other peoples had for putting the wife in her place. For example, English law permits a husband to beat his wife. This crude means of wife-taming is nowhere condoned by Jewish law. One rabbi even declared that a husband who beats his wife should be punished more severely than one who beats his neighbor. He should be chastised in every conceivable way and even excommunicated.

With regard to Jewish divorce, one problem remains unsolved to this day—that of the deserted wife, or *agunah*. The *agunah* is a woman who cannot obtain a bill of divorce from her absent husband because she cannot find him and has no proof that he is dead. She is not permitted to remarry, nor can she sue for divorce on the grounds of desertion as one could do according to most civil law. Sometimes a clause was included in the *ketubah* ensuring the wife's right to a divorce should the husband disappear. But in nearly all cases the woman was placed in the unfortunate position of being a wife and a widow at the same time. Conferences on this subject have been held, but rabbis generally agree that nothing can be done for the *agunah*. It is difficult, however, to understand why the rabbis do not take advantage of their power to annul marriages retroactively. Their failure to do so can only mean that the Jewish court today has lost the power to enforce its dictates.

THE WOMANLY DUTIES

A woman was exempt from all positive time-bound commandments such as reciting the *Shema* (the affirmation of faith) and putting on *tefillin* (phylacteries) in order that she might have sufficient time to raise her family and care for her home. This did not mean that she was prohibited from performing them, but merely that she was not obligated to do so. She *was* obligated with regard to the negative commandments.

Three duties are specifically enjoined upon the Jewish woman. The first of these is kindling the Sabbath lights. This obligation was probably given to her because she is always at home attending to household affairs. Jewish law states that if she neglects to light the Sabbath candles, she must light an extra candle every Friday as long as she lives. The law also states that men as well as women are obliged to light Sabbath candles.

Woman's second obligation is that of taking *hallah* (dough). The Bible commands that the first part of the dough is to be set aside as a sacrifice. In biblical times, it was consecrated to the priests. After the destruction of the Temple, a symbolical sacrifice was offered by taking off a small piece of the dough and throwing it into the fire or burning it in the oven. This was a precept specifically assigned to the mistress of the house, but in her absence anyone could perform it.

The third duty assigned to women concerns the laws of *niddah,* or separation. According to Jewish law, all sexual contact between husband and wife is prohibited during the wife's menstrual period and for seven days after it. Before intercourse can be resumed, the wife must immerse herself in the *mikvah,* or ritual bath. With the development of modern sanitary facilities in the home, a community bath house would seem unnecessary, but traditional Judaism has retained the laws of ritual purity as a symbol of the sanctity of the Jewish home.

POINT OF VIEW

According to the Midrash, a woman who abandons the laws of *niddah* will be punished by death in childbirth. An obvious exploitation of sexual mythology, this is an insult to the dignity of woman. Primitive taboo made the menstruating woman ritually impure and led to the deduction that she was also physically unclean and repulsive. Naturally this had a tremendous psychological effect upon women which adversely affected their self-esteem as well as their attitude toward their own bodies. No wonder so many refer to menstruation as "the curse."

Making the laws of *niddah,* along with lighting Sabbath candles and taking *hallah,* the only duties incumbent upon Jewish women may also threaten the survival of our people. If that's all there is, why shouldn't Jewish women throw up their hands in disgust and say, "Who cares?" No one questions the importance of lighting candles on *Shabbat.* But why shouldn't men also participate in this *mitzvah* (commandment)? As for the laws of *niddah* and taking *hallah,* they seem senseless and irrelevant to modern society. Shouldn't they be replaced with meaningful activities that represent positive Jewish values and encourage increased participation and creativity in the life of the Jewish community?

TALMUDIC SAYINGS

Thus far we have discussed the legal status of women in Talmudic times. To complete the picture, we must also examine the stories the rabbis told about the women who were part of their lives. For example, they considered one of woman's primary responsibilities to provide study time for her husband and sons. The woman who best exemplified this role was Rachel, wife of Rabbi Akiba. She first met her future husband when he was a shepherd for her father's flocks. He was ignorant and unlearned, but she promised to marry him if he would study at the academy among the great rabbis. They married against her father's will, and Akiba left her in poverty to study at the *yeshivah.* Twenty-four years later he returned to her as a renowned scholar and great leader. She was rewarded for her encouragement and devotion when Akiba told his followers that she was responsible for all the knowledge that he had acquired.

Another woman we read about in the Talmud is Ima Shalom. One day a visiting Roman questioned God's integrity, asking why He had stolen a rib from Adam while he was sleeping. Ima Shalom, who possessed a ready wit, asked the man to summon a guard. When he asked why, she replied that a thief had robbed them of a silver cup and left a gold one in its place. The Roman laughed and said that he would be quite happy if a thief left him richer than he had been before. Ima Shalom replied that that was how Adam felt when God took his rib and gave him in return a woman to comfort him in his loneliness.

The wife of Rabbi Meir also deviated from the usual Talmudic description of a woman as lightheaded and prone to gossip. Her name was Beruria, and she was recognized as a scholar in her own right. She participated in legal discussions, and the Talmud records her opinions. Her wisdom is evident from the way in which she informed her husband of the death of their two sons. When he returned home to celebrate the Sabbath, she welcomed him as if no sorrow had befallen them. When he asked for his sons, she said that she would explain their absence after they had finished the Sabbath meal. She then asked his advice in a very important matter.

A stranger who had given her some jewels to take care of, she said, had now returned and demanded that she give the jewels back. She had grown very fond of them and wanted to know if she had to return them. Rabbi Meir was astonished that a woman as wise as his wife would ask such a foolish question, and he replied that certainly she must give them back. At that point Beruria took him into the room where their two sons lay dead and in his grief she comforted him. "They were jewels given to us by God for safekeeping," she said, "until He demanded them for Himself once again."

Other women in the Talmud were praised for their understanding and compassion. A man was cautioned never to hurt his wife's feelings and was reminded that the one who loves his wife as himself and honors her more than himself has divine assurance of domestic peace. According to the rabbis, women had a greater capacity for fidelity than men. In fact, the Israelites were redeemed from Egypt through the merit of the pious women of their generation. The rabbis also said that everything depends on the woman. A pious man who marries a wicked woman becomes wicked, while a wicked man who marries a righteous woman becomes righteous.

But a majority of sayings scorned women in general. They were not permitted to serve as witnesses because of their boldness and levity. They possessed no wisdom except in household activities; therefore it was frivolous to teach them Torah. They brought only anxiety and woe to their fathers. They were willing to marry anyone, even if he was ugly and loathsome, because it was better to be married than to be a spinster. They were not to remain idle, but neither were they to have careers because any home supported by a woman would not enjoy divine blessings.

POINT OF VIEW

When considering sayings recorded in the Talmud, we ought to remember that they were the opinions of individual men. Particular statements of scorn may have been the result of any number of personal hangups on the part of our scholars and sages. Still, it must be seen how wrong it is to implant within a daughter's mind the idea that she must suppress her own ambitions in order that her husband and sons may achieve theirs. This attitude may have contributed to the survival of our people (after all, the argument goes, children are our future and what greater and more important job could there be than to raise them?). Yet it most certainly deprived us of unlimited creativity on the part of women who might have made

significant contributions to humanity, had they been permitted and encouraged to develop their potential to its
fullest. ৯৯

CHAPTER THREE

Emancipation Brings Changes

In the Middle Ages, philosophers and scholars accepted the teachings of the Talmud regarding women. Men were cautioned to honor and respect their wives and to provide adequate care for them. Women were expected to fulfill their household duties and were not encouraged to go beyond their family responsibilities. The academies of learning were closed to them, and according to Maimonides, they were not to hold any communal office.

Women were also barred from studying Jewish mysticism. While the Kabbalists recognized a feminine element in God, they tended to emphasize the demonic nature of women. The female sex represented the quality of strict judgment rather than sensitivity, and Jewish mystics generally believed women to be more heartless, less creative, and less intelligent than men.

On the other hand, Hasidism recognized the vital role of women in Jewish life. Several women were known for their intelligence and respected for their scholarly opinions. Hasidim flocked to Feige, mother of Rabbi Nahman of Bratzlav, to receive her blessings and to Malka, wife of Rabbi Shalom of Belz, to seek her advice. Sarah, daughter of Rabbi Joshua Heshel Teumin Frankel, was so respected that even rabbis sought her counsel. Rabbi Mordecai Twer-

sky considered his daughter, Hannah Havah, equal in piety
to his sons. And the most famous of all Hasidic women was
Hannah Rachel Werbermacher. Known as the "Maid of
Ludmir," she wore *tzitzit* (ritual fringes), wrapped herself
in a *tallit* (prayershawl), and put on *tefillin*. Every *Shabbat*
she preached a sermon attended by rabbis and scholars,
and many referred to her as *"rebbe."* Of course, these
women were exceptions. It was not until the beginning of
Reform Judaism that any major changes in the role of
women were to occur.

EUROPEAN REFORM

With the coming of emancipation in the early nineteenth century, many German Jews believed that religious
reform would ensure their right to freedom. In an attempt
to be more like their neighbors, Jews began introducing
changes into the synagogue service. To enrich worship
esthetically, the traditional male choir was replaced by a
mixed male and female choir and hymns were sung in
German instead of Hebrew. An organ was installed in
the temple and the service shortened. A sermon, preached
in German, became a regular part of worship, and the
weekly Torah portion was read in the Sephardic rather
than the Ashkenazic pronunciation. Confirmation exercises
were instituted, first for boys and soon afterward for girls.
No longer did Jewish worshipers pray for the restoration
of Zion in the homeland of Israel. Instead, they delighted
in their dispersion and pledged their allegiance to the
nation in which they lived, hoping to be given all the
privileges of citizenship.

Women benefited from this desire to modernize religious doctrines and practices. In Frankfort am Main in
July 1845, the Conference of the Rabbis of Germany stated:

One of the marked achievements of the Reform movement has been the change in the status of women. According to the Talmud and the Rabbinic Code, woman can take no part in public religious functions, but this Conference declares that woman has the same obligation as man to participate from youth up in the instruction of Judaism and in the public services and that the custom not to include women in the number of individuals necessary for the conducting of a public service (a *minyan*) is only a custom and has no religious basis.[1]

The Breslau Conference in 1846 granted women total equality:

The *halachic* [legal] position of women must undergo a change, and it is hoped that all members will be unanimous on that subject. . . . [Jewish women] have received assurances of their capabilities for emancipation, without, however, being indeed permitted to become emancipated. It is useless to argue why the religious situation of women has become impaired. . . . To be sure, according to their viewpoint, the rabbis were absolutely right in systematically excluding the female sex from a significant part of religious duties and rights, and the poor woman could not complain about being denied exalted spiritual blessings, for it was believed that God himself had pronounced the damning verdict over her. In the face of so many offending slights in civic life, she could not even complain about the fact that the house of God was as good as closed to her, that she had to beg the rabbi's permission for the daily expression of her Israelitish faith, as one begs for alms. She was permitted a share neither in religious instruction nor in certain sacred parental duties. The execution of sacred acts was now permitted, now forbidden to her; and finally, through the man's daily benediction for the good fortune of not having become a woman, she had to experience the most bitter offense in the very house of God. And yet, all this appears most mild when compared to the conferences of a Christian Council in the Middle Ages, debating whether a woman had a soul at all!

For our religious consciousness . . . it is a sacred duty to express most emphatically the complete religious equality of the female sex. Life, which is stronger than all theory, has indeed achieved quite a bit in this regard; however, a great deal is still lacking for the achievement of absolute equality, and even the little that has occurred already is still devoid of all *halachic* strength. It is thus our task to pronounce the equality of religious privileges and obligations of women in so far as this is possible. We have exactly the same right to do this as the synod under R. Gershom, eight hundred years ago, which also introduced new religious decrees in favor of the female sex. . . .

Esteemed gentlemen, the Committee herewith submits the following proposals for your examination:

The Rabbinical Conference shall declare the female sex as religiously equal with the male, in its obligations and rights, and pronounce accordingly as *halachic:*

1. That women must observe all *mitzvot,* even though they pertain to a certain time, in so far as these *mitzvot* have any strength and vigor at all for our religious consciousness;

2. That the female sex has to fulfill all obligations toward children in the same manner as the male;

3. That neither the husband nor the father has the right to absolve a religiously mature daughter or wife from her vow;

4. That from now on, the benediction *shelo assani ishah* (who has not made me a woman), which was the basis for the religious prejudice against women, shall be abolished;

5. That the female sex shall, from earliest youth, be obligated to participate in religious instruction and public worship, and in the latter respect also be counted in a *minyan;* and finally,

6. That the religious coming of age for both sexes begin with the age of thirteen.[2]

POINT OF VIEW

Judging from the language of this resolution, its authors probably thought that they were eliminating all discrimination against women. But there were other areas in which they failed to take action. No mention was made of the separate seating in synagogues, in which women were relegated to the gallery. Nothing was said about the special burdensome duties that women were obligated to observe. No encouragement was given to women to seek leadership roles within the synagogue structure. Women would have to wait for these changes, but at least the first step had been taken.

AMERICAN REFORM

Soon after Reform Judaism was introduced in Germany it spread to America, where it was to exert a considerable impact. Under the leadership of Isaac Mayer Wise and others, new reforms were instituted. The custom of selling *aliyot* (being called to read from Torah) was eliminated and the observance of the second day of the festivals discontinued. Men were no longer required to wear a *tallit* and *kipah* (skullcap) when they worshiped. Families were permitted to sit together during services and a new prayerbook was adopted. Wise was determined to discard the minute regulations which he felt impeded the progress of Judaism and to allow individuals to decide for themselves, through reason and conscience, which customs and ceremonies should be observed.

Once again, women benefited from this revolt against tradition. On July 10, 1892, the Central Conference of American Rabbis adopted the following resolution:

> Whereas we have progressed beyond the idea of a secondary position of women in Jewish congregations,

we recognize the importance of their hearty cooperation and active participation in congregational affairs; therefore be it resolved that women be eligible to full membership with all the privileges of voting and holding office in our congregations.[3]

Isaac Mayer Wise was himself one of the greatest supporters of equal rights for women. He offered to appear in any congregation to plead their case:

In the early days of our activity in America, we admitted females to the choir. Then we confirmed boys and girls together, and we allowed girls to read the Torah on that occasion. Later on we introduced family pews into the Temple.

With the admission of mothers and daughters to a recognized place in public worship, came order and decorum. Abuses that had crept into the synagogue disappeared as soon as woman again took her proper place in the Temple. But we cannot stop here; the reform is not complete. You must enfranchise woman in your congregations, she must be a member, must have a voice and a vote in your assemblies. We need women in the congregational boards to bring heart and piety into them. We must have women in the boards for the sake of the principle. We must have women in the school boards to visit the Sabbath schools, and to make their influence felt. We must have women in the choir committees, because they understand music better than men. But, all other considerations aside, the principle of justice, and the law of God inherent in every human being, demand that woman be admitted to membership in the congregation, and be given equal rights with man; that her religious feelings be allowed scope for the sacred cause of Israel.

We are ready to appear before any congregation in behalf of any woman wishing to become a member thereof, and to plead her cause. We will debate the question with anyone who will show us in what woman is less entitled to the privileges of the synagogue than the man, or where her faith is less important to her salvation than man's is to him. Till then, we must maintain that women must become active members of the congregation for their own sake, and for the benefit of Israel's sacred cause.[4]

POINT OF VIEW

The spirit was there, but the attitudes of people have to be changed in order to transform reality. And in many cases we are just beginning to do that. While most congregations have granted women the privileges of membership and voting, only about 5 percent of all Reform congregations have women serving as presidents and vice-presidents. And only about 4 percent of the members of the Board of Trustees of the Union of American Hebrew Congregations are women. If we are serious about granting women equality, then we had better abide by our resolutions. The time has come to conquer our own psychological and emotional objections and to regard every human being as a real person with talents and skills and with the option of contributing to the betterment of the congregation in any way she or he finds meaningful. Those who are unwilling to do so should return to the fold of Orthodoxy, for in all good conscience they cannot consider themselves liberal Jews.

CONSERVATIVE JUDAISM

Conservative Judaism developed mainly in response to the needs of those who found Orthodoxy too rigid and Reform too lax for the expression of their religious beliefs. While Conservative Jews accept the authority of tradition, they generally agree that change is an essential feature of religion; therefore, *Halachah* (traditional Jewish law) must be adapted to the prevailing conditions of life in the Jewish community. The Rabbinical Assembly is officially charged with this awesome task. Any changes which are to be made concerning the position of women must come from the rabbis themselves.

Recognizing this fact, a group of women who call themselves *Ezrat Nashim* distributed the following statement to those attending the Rabbinical Assembly Convention in 1972:

> The Jewish tradition regarding women, once far ahead of other cultures, has now fallen disgracefully behind in failing to come to terms with developments of the past century.
>
> Accepting the age-old concept of role differentiation on the basis of sex, Judaism saw woman's role as that of wife, mother, and homemaker. Her ritual obligations were domestic and familial: *nerot, hallah,* and *taharat ha-mishpahah* [candles, dough, family purity]. Although the woman was extolled for her domestic achievements, and respected as the foundation of the Jewish family, she was never permitted an active role in the synagogue, court, or house of study. These limitations on the life-patterns open to women, appropriate or even progressive for the rabbinic and medieval periods, are entirely unacceptable to us today.
>
> The social position and self-image of women have changed radically in recent years. It is now universally accepted that women are equal to men in intellectual capacity, leadership ability, and spiritual depth. The Conservative movement has tacitly acknowledged this fact by demanding that their female children be educated alongside the males—up to the level of rabbinical school. To educate women and deny them the opportunity to act from this knowledge is an affront to their intelligence, talents, and integrity.
>
> As products of Conservative congregations, religious schools, the Ramah camps, LTF, USY, and the seminary, we feel this tension acutely. We are deeply committed to Judaism, but cannot find adequate expression for our total needs and concerns in existing women's social and charitable organizations. Furthermore, the single woman—a new reality in Jewish life—is almost

totally excluded from the organized Jewish community, which views women solely as daughters, wives, and mothers. The educational institutions of the Conservative moment have helped women recognize their intellectual, social, and spiritual potential. If the movement then denies women opportunities to demonstrate these capacities as adults, it will force them to turn from the synagogue, and to find fulfillment elsewhere.

It is not enough to say that Judaism views women as separate but equal, nor to point to Judaism's past superiority over other cultures in its treatment of women. We've had enough of apologetics: enough of Beruria, Deborah, and Esther; enough of *"ayshet hayil"* ("woman of valor").

It is time that:

Women be granted membership in synagogues

Women be counted in the *minyan*

Women be allowed full participation in religious observances—*aliyot, baalot keriah* [readers of Torah], *shleehot tzibbur* [leaders of prayer]

Women be recognized as witnesses before Jewish law

Women be allowed to initiate divorce

Women be permitted and encouraged to attend rabbinical and cantorial schools, and to perform rabbinical and cantorial functions in synagogues

Women be encouraged to join decisionmaking bodies, and to assume professional leadership roles, in synagogues and in the general Jewish community

Women be considered as bound to fulfill all *mitzvot* equally with men

For three thousand years, one-half of the Jewish people have been excluded from full participation in Jewish communal life. We call for an end to the second-class status of women in Jewish life.

Nothing could better express the feelings and frustrations of modern Jewish women who seek meaningful and full participation within the Jewish community than this very personal statement by *Ezrat Nashim*. These women have recognized that change will not come until it is demanded by women themselves. As a result of their continued prodding, members of the Rabbinical Assembly agreed in 1974 to count women in the *minyan* and to allow women to participate in the ritual aspects of the synagogue. They are also studying the matter of ordination of women.

RECONSTRUCTIONISM

Reconstructionism is an offshoot of Conservative Judaism and represents an attempt, primarily by Mordecai M. Kaplan, to provide a clear and precise ideology for American Jews. Kaplan called for a complete reevaluation of the status of women in Jewish life and addressed himself concretely to the task of granting them full participation. He instituted the ceremony of *Bat Mitzvah,* giving girls the opportunity to observe the same ritual procedures followed by boys when celebrating their *Bar Mitzvah.* He advocated counting women in the *minyan* and giving them *aliyot.* In 1968 he helped to found the Reconstructionist Rabbinical College, which encouraged the admission of women, and in 1974 Rabbi Sandy Eisenberg Sasso was ordained as the first Reconstructionist woman rabbi.

Kaplan's words speak for themselves:

Few aspects of Jewish thought and life illustrate so strikingly the need of reconstructing Jewish law as the traditional status of the Jewish woman. In Jewish tradition, her status is unquestionably that of inferiority to the man. If the Jewish woman is to contribute her share to the regeneration of Jewish life, and if in turn Jewish life is to bring out the powers for good that are in her, this status must be changed. She must attain in Jewish law and practice a position of religious, civic, and juridicial equality with the man, and this attainment must come about by her own efforts and initiative. Whatever liberal-minded men do in her behalf is bound to remain a futile and meaningless gesture. The Jewish woman must demand the equality due her as a right to which she is fully entitled. . . . There is no reason why the Jewish civilization should persist in treating her in this day and age as though she were an inferior type of human being.[5]

POINT OF VIEW

The position of women has undergone radical change in recent years. Society has finally recognized that women are equal to men and that they too possess intellectual skill, ambition, the ability to lead, and the capacity for profound spiritual expression. Although women are entering new fields every day, this transformation in social structure is far from complete, particularly within the religious community. If we are serious about granting women equal rights, then we must not only welcome their participation, but heartily encourage and urge women to take new roles within organized religion. If we fail to do so, we deprive ourselves and future generations of their wisdom, creativity, and experience even as we waste invaluable human potential. Judaism has taken the lead before. Let us provide a light once again.

CHAPTER FOUR

Creation of the State of Israel

WOMEN PIONEERS

Jewish men and women who came to Palestine as pioneers brought with them a firm commitment to the reestablishment of the Jewish homeland. Persecuted Jews were at last to know freedom, and that meant freedom for all—women and men. Women, who had suffered the degradation of inferior status in every class and society, had a right to suppose that they too would be liberated. They expected to work side by side with the men in all phases of labor, not to be told that a woman's place is in the kitchen. They faced stubborn opposition, however:

> "We believed that the wall which divided man's work from woman's had fallen forever," cries Miriam Schlimovitch reproachfully. "I remembered," says another *halutzah* [woman pioneer], "that before setting out for Palestine I had worked everywhere in the *halutz* organization—the preparatory schools for pioneers in Europe—on a footing of absolute equality with the men. In time, I used to think, we will establish the same equality in Palestine. But when I got here I could not stand the amused irony, the patronizing superior attitude of the stronger toward the weaker. . . . The whole struggle seemed to me a fantastic thing. I asked myself: Have the men forgotten the time—it was only yester-

day—when they too were unskilled? And aren't there among the men the strong and the weak, the efficient and the inefficient? Why the hostile attitude from the outset toward the woman worker?" [1]

The women pioneers realized that they would have to write their own chapter in Jewish history, for there were simply no working women in Palestine at the beginning of the twentieth century. As can be expected, it was not easy for them to find jobs. They were usually assigned to the kitchen. But they did not remain silent in the face of this discrimination. At one of the workers' conferences, it was suggested that girls be sought to increase the number of kitchen workers. Yael Gordon, one of the feminist pioneers, replied:

> We women agree with you completely that we must try to bring more girls into our workers' groups; however, not because we need more hands in the kitchen, but because women must be partners in the revival of our people. It is true that only a few girls have so far tried to engage in heavy manual labor, but the reason for this is the scorn with which their efforts were greeted. This attitude is completely unjustified and will have to change. When it does, many girls will come to work in the fields and elsewhere. No man has the right to tell them beforehand that they will be restricted to the kitchen. They will find work for themselves of their own free choice. [2]

These women were determined to share equally in rebuilding the land. They established training farms where girls could learn about vegetable growing, poultry raising, dairying, cooking, and household management. They hoped that training on these farms would lead to improved work relations between men and women.

By 1914, women were formally organized in Palestine. Their aim was expressed by Yael Gordon:

We want full equality and real emancipation so that women may function effectively both as individuals and as members of the group! We look forward to achieving this in the new society now being created in the land of Israel out of our people's desire to preserve its individuality through work and creativity. The girls who have come here have done so as members of our people, dedicated to carrying out their national duties, but they wish also to find themselves, their individuality, as women and as human beings. This small laboring society of ours is the best place on earth in which to discover the roots of one's soul.[3]

During World War I at least four conferences were held in Palestine for working women. One of the questions constantly discussed was the care of children on communal settlements, or *kvutzot*. Some mothers wanted to care for their own children; others believed that *kvutzah* life demanded communal care. Those who were totally committed to this revolutionary kind of living were convinced that child care had to be collective. Otherwise people might demand private gardens or private kitchens or private chickens. If the *kvutzah* was to be successful, then child care would have to be communal as was every other activity. Only then would women have the freedom to perform the necessary agricultural tasks and to participate fully in the life of the settlement.

Agriculture was not the only field in which women worked; they were involved in every phase of building up the country. The story of "Techiah," one of the early members of the Council of Working Women, is typical of the problems women faced:

For the first time . . . thousands of Jews had entered the building trade and had mastered it. And the Jewish woman worker began to batter at the doors of the trade. But it was not so easy to get in.

The men had quite a number of reasons for keeping

us out. Some said the work was too strenuous for women. Others argued that if women were admitted into the building trade collectives . . . the output would decrease and the pay with it. The fight went on for quite a time, and finally the workers of Tel Aviv decided that every building trade collective had to admit two women.

I knew that I was being received not spontaneously, but under orders. . . . I wanted therefore to give up my right to enter the building collective, but friends of mine in the Council of Women Workers persuaded me to hold on. Just because the men looked at it as they did, it was my duty to go in, and to try and create a new relationship. . . .

At five o'clock I reported. My place was with the cement workers. I stood by and poured on water while the men mixed. The mixture when ready was carried over to the building place in buckets on planks.

They worked slowly at first, yesterday's weariness still being in their limbs. Gradually the work livened up. Gradually I too was caught up in the rhythm of it. . . . But in comparison with the tasks of the men, mine was a trifling one, and I felt the slight. . . .

So I changed off with one of the men, and began to carry cement. The comrade who loaded the cement on to the plank said, "That's all right. Let her lift this a couple of times—she'll be asking for something easier."

And I must confess that the load nearly made me stagger. But I called up all my will power and walked with steady steps, as if this was the most usual thing for me. I knew a dozen pairs of eyes were watching me slyly, and if I faltered once there would be a shout of laughter.

Later I noticed that the comrade who did the loading was putting more on my plank than on anyone else's. I understood and said nothing. After a while I stood still and looked at him with a smile. He became confused. The comrade who carried the plank with me kept complaining that it was too heavy. He wondered how on earth I could lift my end, and became angry with the loader. But I asked him to keep quiet and wait. I was right. The next time the load was considerably lighter, and the loader got his share of abuse from the others.

The same story was repeated when it came to filling in the foundations. And in this way a fight went on between me and a couple of them, all day long, until I forced them to give way. The next day they confessed that instead of getting a laugh at my expense, they had learned to respect me.

My reputation as a good worker was soon established. . . . When the elections came around for the council of the building workers, my name was put up.

There isn't very much to this story. . . . I only tell it to help make clear the struggle which the women workers of Palestine had to wage when trying to break into a new field.[4]

POINT OF VIEW

Undoubtedly, women have to face similar obstacles whenever they enter a field that has previously been open only to men. They are forced to be better than everyone else, to possess unlimited patience, and to accept whatever happens. When they do not, and when they respond too vocally or too angrily (regardless of whether or not their response is justifiable), they generally run the risk of losing the respect which is almost always forthcoming. That respect is an important aspect of the struggle for equal rights, because respect brings acceptance.

Another common situation which women have to face in the struggle for emancipation arose when *Haboneh*, Palestine's largest contracting agency, suddenly dismissed the ten women it had hired. When the women demanded an explanation,

the director held a whispered conversation with his assistant and then answered haltingly: "It's true that your work was quite all right. But is it your aim in life to be construction workers? Can we depend on you to stay? You are going to get married and stop working. The men are different. We hope to train them to be good masons. But we have no need for women here. . . ."

The girls were overwhelmed. They had never thought about what their "aim" was. They had come to Palestine to work—quite simply, without any ulterior motives. And what business was it of the director's to worry about their futures? [5]

Society unfairly assumed that women had to choose between families and careers. Isn't it about time that we affirm a woman's right to do both?

Still another problem arose in families where both the husband and wife were employed. In times of crisis and unemployment, it was recommended that one partner (preferably the woman) stop working. Those who favored women's rights vigorously opposed this suggestion. David Ben Gurion expressed their opinion:

Forbidding couples to work, as a blanket rule, will have a strong adverse effect on the right to work and the independence of women. A woman, even when she is married, has every right to be economically independent, i.e. to support herself, and not be dependent on her husband.

Our movement is fighting for the rights of the permanently employed worker. It would not occur to anyone to make a ruling that upon his marriage a man be dismissed from his place of work. It is only the stereotyped thinking of society in which women are oppressed and without rights that makes it possible for us to discriminate between working men and women with respect to tenure.

It is well known that job opportunities open to women are fewer than those open to men. If a law is passed stating that married women must leave their jobs, we will be undermining the very foundations of our movement. Employers will then have new reason to follow the trend, which is strong in any case, of preventing women from securing employment.

Differences in standards of living within the working public are not caused solely by the work of married couples. Individual laborers and white collar workers (and their female counterparts) do not receive equal salaries, and there are cases where the joint wages of a working couple are smaller than those of a single man working on his own.[6]

With David Ben Gurion on their side, how could women lose?

CONSCIOUSNESS-RAISING

Despite strong support for the movement to establish equal rights, it was still necessary to raise the consciousness of many women.

The Working Women's Council was particularly concerned with the level of the wages paid to women: these were always considerably lower than those paid to men in similar jobs. Raising the wage scale of women would, the Council felt, not only help them economically but increase their self-respect and make them feel that they were not "second class" citizens. There were some very difficult psychological problems involved: it would have been much easier to achieve wage increases for women if they had been more persistent in their devotion to the occupations in which they managed to gain entry. In periods of unemployment they would go from one job to another and, after the crisis passed, would show no inclination to return to their original job. Lack of persistence naturally led to lack of specialization and skill, and this in turn contributed to the lower wage scale. Similarly, many women did not understand the importance of belonging to a trade union, despite the fact that they were often obviously exploited and in need of protection. Much work still remained to be done to awaken their trade-union consciousness and organize them effectively.[7]

Women often felt incapable of running for public office. As a result, very few women were elected as delegates to important conferences.

> Perhaps the fault lies with women themselves. They shrink from appearing on public platforms: they are always afraid that what they want to say may not be important or has already been said by someone else in one form or another. What is more, when a woman does get up in public and is somewhat inarticulate (just as scores of men are), her individual failure is at once held against women as a group. If, however, a woman discusses a subject cogently, the general reaction is that "she is an exception to the rule." For this reason women generally remain silent in public assemblies, the habit gradually becoming second nature. This self-imposed silence is bound to hamper their intellectual development, for the ability to think increases with the efforts to express ideas, whether orally or in writing. This being the case, special importance attaches to the meetings and conferences organized by the working women which have always served them as an excellent training ground, helping them to attain self-confidence and become aware of their places in society. Our pioneering women understood this from the very inception of the movement.[8]

Don't we see the same thing happening in our congregations and classrooms today?

CHANGES IN THE LAW

In the State of Israel, Orthodox Jewish law prevails. As we have seen, this usually causes women to be treated like second-class citizens in certain respects. As the social status of Israeli women improved, legal equality was also demanded. Changes were necessary, and women themselves took the initiative in insisting upon them.

Representatives of the feminist movement argued that, where economic matters were concerned, Jewish religious authorities have found ways to reinterpret the law in the light of changing conditions, but in matters pertaining to the family, and especially where women's rights were concerned, strict legalism has ever been the rule. In the final analysis, perhaps the Jewish women's passive acceptance of masculine rule was to blame for this situation. Now, however, women are demanding their rights and will no longer tolerate such treatment. Our new State needs the talents and energies of all its citizens—women included. . . .

At the close of the debate, one of the women delegates proclaimed from the rostrum: "A rabbinate which seeks to uphold the integrity of Judaism ought to evolve necessary legal reforms instead of leaving the law in its petrified form which is humiliating for Jewish women." Women in Israel ought to take the initiative in demanding such reforms, so that they may live in dignity according to the law.[9]

Women accepted the challenge, and the first major reform came on June 6, 1951, when the *Knesset* (parliament) passed the Child Marriage Act. This law raised the minimum marriage age from fifteen to seventeen. It served most especially to protect young Oriental girls from being married off by their fathers before they were emotionally and mentally capable of marriage. Under terms of the law, parents, guardians, husbands, and rabbis are subject to up to two years' imprisonment plus a fine of up to 600 Israeli pounds for violating the law. Even though the penalties are severe, the marriage itself remains valid under Israel's religious law unless the husband consents to a divorce. The real effectiveness of the law, then, is its power to protect child-brides rather than repair damage already done.

A second major reform was the Women's Equal Rights Bill passed on July 17, 1951. It read in part:

1. A man and a woman shall have equal status with regard to any legal proceedings; any provision of law which discriminates, with regard to any legal proceeding, against women as women, shall be of no effect.

2. A married woman shall be fully competent to own and deal with property as if she were unmarried; her rights in property acquired before her marriage shall not be affected by her marriage.

3. (a) Both parents are the natural guardians of their children; where one parent dies, the survivor shall be the natural guardian.[10]

In addition, this law demanded consent of both husband and wife before a divorce could be granted.

According to traditional law, the husband alone has the power of divorce. It is true that the eleventh century *takkanah* (amendment) of Rabbi Gershom of Mayence required the wife's consent to the divorce. This reform, however, was never accepted by the Sephardic community. Morover, the law could be circumvented simply by the husband's threat to abandon his wife, in which case the law of the *agunah* forbade her ever to remarry.

Under the terms of the new Women's Equal Rights Law, both parties must give their consent to the divorce. Men leaving their wives without mutual agreement or without the consent of the court are subject to imprisonment up to five years. Where the husband leaves the jurisdiction of the court, the court itself may issue the *get* or bill of divorcement.[11]

Not every reform futhered the cause of women's liberation. In 1953 a Law of National Service watered down the 1949 Law of Military Service, which required every woman between the ages of eighteen and thirty-four to enlist in the army for a period of two years. The 1953 law exempted four classes of women from military service: married women, women who have children, pregnant women, and women who claim religious beliefs as a basis for exemption. Those of the latter category had to fulfill their national obligation in one of three ways: (1) agricultural training in a religious settlement of their choice; (2) working for the army outside the military establishment, not in military uniform, but at army salaries; or (3) engaging in work of national importance, such as taking care of new immigrants and their children, or school or health work, at army salaries. On the surface this law appears to protect women, but in reality it deprives them of equal responsibilities and rewards them instead for getting married and having children.

ISRAEL TODAY

As we have seen, women have played an important role in the creation of the State of Israel. In every sphere they have challenged discrimination and proved themselves equal to men. They have fought for the right to use their own talents and skills in ways they find meaningful and have made significant contributions to the rebuilding of the land. They have been involved in the development of *kibbutz* (collective settlement) life and have assisted in the formation of the Federation of Labor. They have stood ready to fight in times of war and to build in times of peace. But what of the Israeli woman today? Is she as liberated as her sisters were in the first half of the century?

Apparently the position of the Israeli woman has regressed in recent years. Once the state was established and the pioneering days were over, working women were no longer needed. The religious authorities took over and emphasized their belief that a woman's place is in the home. This has led to discrimination against women with regard to income tax, pension laws, and national insurance programs. In a recent article, Shulamit Aloni, one of the few female members of the *Knesset,* discussed one of the problems facing working women:

The cost of hiring household help for working mothers is not tax deductible. Women who demanded such a tax allowance were told by the Income Tax Department: "Your compensation is the satisfaction you get from working outside the home." As if this is a right a woman doesn't have coming to her, and as if her sole duty is to launder diapers and scour pots. Why do ministers, judges, and other people feel they are entitled to financial compensation but that the working mother is not? The stock answer is: because her place is first and foremost in the home raising her children and serving her husband. This is "the Law of Nature."

That outlook has resulted in guilt feelings and tension among women who have kept on working, while those who quit when they are pregnant do not return to the labor market, even though their lack of fulfillment from housework does not make them better wives or mothers. Social pressure and the fact that taking a job doesn't pay have encouraged them to stay at home, generally to their husbands' satisfaction. The men are quite happy to release their wives from duties and responsibilities because they are at the same time divesting them of their rights.[12]

Ms. Aloni blames women themselves for this turn of events. The Working Women's Council carries little political weight today, compared to its power thirty years ago. Had it retained its influence and demanded the fulfillment of the promises made when the state was created, working mothers would not have many of the problems they are faced with and religious law would have been changed by now. But the leadership of the council has been content to rest on the achievements of a former generation.

Ms. Aloni sees hope for the future, however:

There is still time to reverse the great retreat which has set us back almost without our realizing it. We should constantly work at influencing our subconscious, for one thing. And the Israeli woman does not have to demonstrate in the streets, lobby the legislature, or utter whoops of rebellion. She merely needs to know the rights given to her by the laws of the land and to want to exercise those rights. We will have to rewrite the schoolbooks and remove the classic pictures of "father sitting in the armchair reading the paper while mother bakes bread with the child hanging on her apron," as well as dare to do away with some of the sacred cows the male religious establishment has injected into morality and legislation as the "will of God."

The difference lies not in nature, heredity, or biology —it is merely the product of education, culture, and the consensus of society.

But a woman must always remember that there can be no rights without responsibilities. Our tragedy is that we ourselves have been perfectly happy to be rid of duties and responsibilities and to forfeit our rights. It's a hard decision and one which women avoid making when society does not expect or demand it of them.[13]

2

SYNAGOGUE
AND
COMMUNITY

CHAPTER FIVE
Ritual

It is not unusual that so many women feel alienated from the Jewish community. All one has to do is look around the synagogue and see the noticeable lack of female participation. For thousands of years, ritual has been a man's privilege. Women who may have wanted to lead the community in prayer or to function as rabbis and cantors were made to feel that their desires were Jewishly unfeminine. Some ritual aspects of the synagogue have obviously discouraged female participation.

WOMEN AND THE MINYAN

Until recently, women were not counted in the *minyan,* the quorum of ten necessary for public worship. In Numbers 14:27, we read: "How long shall I bear with this evil congregation, that keep murmuring against Me?" The Talmud comments that the word "congregation" refers to the ten scouts who were sent to spy out the land of Canaan and who returned with an unfavorable report. Thus, the custom arose of requiring ten men to constitute a congregation. Others see the origin of the *minyan* in Exodus 18:25 where Moses chose rulers of thousands, of hundreds, of fifties, and of tens to judge the people. Since ten heads of families made up the smallest political subdivision, ten men had to be present before public worship could begin. Whatever the origin, the fact remains that only men were to be counted in the *minyan*.

When a woman came to public worship services (usually only on *Shabbat*), she was not permitted to sit with her husband. She sat either in a balcony or in the back of the room behind a partition. Some attribute this practice to Temple times, when there was a separate Court of the Women. There appears to be no legal basis for it, however, either in the Talmud or in subsequent legal codes. Others say this separation of the sexes was a precaution against the possible occurrence of distraction. A woman was worthy to take part in public worship, but her presence might arouse passion in the male members of the congregation, thereby distracting them from the act of prayer.

THE READING OF TORAH

Contrary to popular belief, a woman *is* permitted to read from the Torah. The Talmud states: "All are qualified to be among the seven (who read), even a minor and a woman, only the sages said that a woman should not read in the Torah out of respect for the congregation (Megillah 23a)." Why "out of respect"? If a woman read, it usually meant that there was no man in the congregation qualified to do so. Thus, the men were shamed.

The common prohibition against women reading from the Torah is also related to the concept that a woman is ritually unclean during her menstrual period. Rather than embarrass her by asking if she is menstruating, it is better, according to the sages, to say that she *never* can read from the Torah. However, there is a contrary view in the Talmud. "It has been taught: R. Judah b. Bathyra used to say: Words of Torah are not susceptible of uncleanness . . . as it says, 'Is not My word like as fire' (Jer. 23:29).

Just as fire is not susceptible of uncleanness, so words of Torah are not susceptible of uncleanness (Ber. 22a)."

LITURGY

The distinction between male and female is further emphasized in the traditional liturgy. Each morning the Orthodox Jew prays, "Praised are You, O Lord our God, King of the Universe, who has not created me a woman." These words have caused a great deal of controversy and discussion among advocates of the feminist movement.

To understand the prayer, we must first understand the concept of *mitzvah*. According to Jewish tradition, a *mitzvah* (commandment) is a privilege. It means additional responsibility and greater efforts, but it also gives one the opportunity to serve God in a prescribed and special way. For example, members of the priestly class (*Cohanim*) were expected to observe certain *mitzvot* that were not required of other Jews. As a result, a priest expressed his gratitude to God for this added privilege by reciting an appropriate blessing. This did not mean that he was better than anyone else; it merely allowed him to give thanks for the special *mitzvot* of priests.

Similarly, a man recites the above blessing in order to express gratitude for the opportunity to observe the commandments, many of which women were not required to keep because of other equally important responsibilities. Commentators have emphasized that this blessing was not intended to downgrade women nor to grant men superiority.

POINT OF VIEW

During the Middle Ages a special blessing was added to the liturgy for women. "Praised are You, O Lord our God, King of the Universe, who has made me according to His will." This alternate wording was an attempt to grant women full participation in public worship. While the original blessing should not be overinterpreted, neither should we ignore the "separate but equal" implications of this substitute version. Our attitude toward women is very different from that of our ancestors. Orthodox Jews should follow the lead of Conservative Jews, who thank God for "making me an Israelite," or Reform Jews, who have removed this blessing from their liturgy altogether.   ᘛ

B'RIT MILAH

Even as worship was male-oriented, so were customs and ceremonies related to the life-cycle. A baby boy is circumcised and named on the eighth day of his life in the ceremony called *B'rit Milah*. The *B'rit* is a symbol of the covenant first made between Abraham and God when Abraham agreed to observe the divine commandments. Through circumcision, baby boys are welcomed into the Jewish tradition and the covenant is passed from father to son in every generation. In contrast to the joyous home celebration that generally accompanies this ceremony, baby girls are named in the synagogue with much less fanfare. Their fathers are given the honor of being called to the Torah and a prayer is recited for the health of mother and child.

PIDYON HABEN

When the firstborn child of a woman is a boy, the ceremony called *Pidyon HaBen* is observed. According to the Bible, the firstborn belongs to God. To most heathen nations, this meant the sacrificial slaying of the firstborn, but to the Jews it meant consecration. The firstborn son received the birthright and was granted the role of leadership. After the exodus from Egypt, Aaron and his sons were consecrated as spiritual leaders, priests. In the ceremony of *Pidyon HaBen,* to symbolize the transferral of leadership from the firstborn to the priest, the father redeems his son by giving five pieces of silver to the priest or, as is most common today, to charity. The ceremony is held on the thirty-first day following birth and is performed only when the boy is the firstborn child of the mother. In other words, it is not performed if a girl has preceded a boy in birth.

BAR MITZVAH

The ceremony of *Bar Mitzvah* evolved in the late Middle Ages and marked the passage of a thirteen-year-old boy into adult life. Afterward the boy was expected to observe all the 613 *mitzvot.* As we have already seen, women were exempt from many of the *mitzvot* and so there was no need for a similar ceremony to mark a girl's passage into adult life.

The essential features of the *Bar Mitzvah* ceremony were the putting on of *tefillin* and being called up to the Torah as one of the seven men called every Sabbath. Because these observances were no longer of prime importance, Reform Judaism at first discarded *Bar Mitzvah* and replaced it with Confirmation.

CONFIRMATION

Originally, Confirmation took place in Reform religious schools and was limited to boys only. It was later transferred to the synagogue and girls were included. It took place on a special Sabbath, such as the Sabbath during Passover or Hanukkah, and only gradually became linked with Shavuot. Today, it gives young men and women the opportunity to publicly commit themselves to a Jewish way of life and to take their places among the people of Israel.

In recent years, many Reform congregations have reinstituted the ceremony of *Bar Mitzvah* and, following the example of the Reconstructionist movement, have added the ceremony of *Bat Mitzvah* for girls. This represents an attempt to grant equal recognition to girls for their accomplishments in religious education and to allow them full participation in the life of the synagogue.

MARRIAGE

Marriage is the next life-cycle event in the life of the Jew. In earlier times (see Chapter Two), marriage was a business transaction. For this reason, a traditional Jewish wedding is never a double-ring ceremony. Only the groom gives a ring, as a symbol of the purchase. Usually it is a simple gold band, the value of which can be easily recognized. This eliminates any possibility of deception.

The wedding ceremony is performed under a *huppah*, or canopy. This symbolizes the marriage chamber in which the bride and groom were united. When a bride joins her groom under the *huppah*, it officially marks her departure from her father's house and her entrance into the house of her husband.

DEATH

The last of the life-cycle events is death. Both men and women are expected to observe traditional mourning customs. Only men, however, are obligated to recite *Kaddish*. This mourner's prayer, which does not mention death but praises the God of life, is to be said by the closest male relative if no sons, brothers, or father survive. In cases where there is no male relative, it is customary to hire someone to recite *Kaddish*. While women are not required to recite this mourner's prayer, they are not prohibited from doing so when attending services in the synagogue. In fact, in many synagogues the entire congregation rises to recite *Kaddish* together.

In 1916, Henrietta Szold expressed her views concerning the obligation to recite *Kaddish* in a letter to a friend:

> It is impossible for me to find words in which to tell you how deeply I was touched by your offer to act as "*Kaddish*" for my dear mother. I cannot even thank you—it is something that goes beyond thanks. It is beautiful, what you have offered to do—I shall never forget it.
>
> You will wonder, then, that I cannot accept your offer. Perhaps it would be best for me not to try to explain to you in writing, but to wait until I see you to tell you why it is so. I know well, and appreciate what you say about, the Jewish custom; and Jewish custom is very dear and sacred to me. And yet I cannot ask you to say *Kaddish* after my mother. The *Kaddish* means to me that the survivor publicly and markedly manifests his wish and intention to assume the relation to the Jewish community which his parent had, and that so the chain of tradition remains unbroken from generation to generation, each adding its own link. You can do that for the generations of your family, I must do that for the generations of my family.
>
> I believe that the elimination of women from such duties was never intended by our law and custom—women were freed from positive duties when they could not perform them, but not when they could. It was never intended that, if they could perform them, their performance of them should not be considered as valuable and valid as when one of the male sex performed them. And of the *Kaddish* I feel sure this is particularly true.

My mother had eight daughters and no son; and yet never did I hear a word of regret pass the lips of either my mother or my father that one of us was not a son. When my father died, my mother would not permit others to take her daughters' place in saying the *Kaddish,* and so I am sure I am acting in her spirit when I am moved to decline your offer. But beautiful your offer remains nevertheless, and, I repeat, I know full well that it is much more in consonance with the generally accepted Jewish tradition than is my or my family's tradition. You understand me, don't you?[1]

ORDINATION OF WOMEN

There is nothing in Jewish law that specifically prohibits the ordination of women as rabbis. Tradition simply did not allow it. As we have noted, however, Reform Judaism established complete equality beween men and women with regard to religious observance. In keeping with this principle, the Central Conference of American Rabbis (CCAR) issued the following statement in 1922:

> The ordination of woman as rabbi is a modern issue, due to the evolution in her status in our day. The Central Conference of American Rabbis has repeatedly made pronouncement urging the fullest measure of self-expression for woman, as well as the fullest utilization of her gifts in the service of the Most High, and gratefully acknowledges the enrichment and enlargement of congregational life which has resulted therefrom.
>
> Whatever may have been the specific legal status of Jewish woman regarding certain religious functions, her general position in Jewish religious life has ever been an exalted one. She has been the priestess in the home, and our sages recognized her as the preserver of Israel. In view of these Jewish teachings and in keeping with the spirit of our age and the traditions of our Conference, we declare that woman cannot justly be denied the privilege of ordination.[2]

In 1956, a committee formed to consider the ordination of women reaffirmed this resolution and urged that the Hebrew Union College-Jewish Institute of Religion admit female rabbinical students. It further recommended that any woman who satisfactorily completed the prescribed course of study be ordained and accepted as a member of the CCAR.

Martha Neumark was the first woman rabbinical candidate at the Hebrew Union College. In 1925, *The Jewish Tribune* published some of her thoughts:

> I have always wondered why I was imbued with the idea of becoming a rabbi. The first distinct recollection I have of a definite feeling toward communal work is connected with my confirmation service. I was one of those who read from the *Torah* in Hebrew, and the recitation of those ancient words crystallized a vague restlessness of mine into a desire to serve my people. The easiest way to enter that field was to enter the Hebrew Union College and become a rabbi! My youthful impetuosity was not concerned with the difficulties of such an undertaking. The doubt never entered my mind as to whether I, a girl, would be ordained. I wanted to serve Judaism and Jews. What other requisite was necessary for admission to the rabbinate?[3]

The Board of Governors did not agree with Martha Neumark—or with the CCAR, for that matter. Eight members were present at the meeting where the question of women in the rabbinate was discussed. The two rabbis who were there voted in favor of the ordination of women; the remaining six members voted against.

Martha Neumark left the Hebrew Union College and her rabbinical studies in the middle of her junior year after almost eight years of study. She felt, nonetheless, that women were probably better fitted for the rabbinate than men. She suggested that congregations hire a male rabbi and a female rabbi and divide the responsibilities between them. After all, men and women compose a congregation; why shouldn't men and women serve a congregation's needs? She emphasized the need for a change in attitude:

> The present attitude of some of the laity is to be regretted, in view of the fact that woman rabbis will benefit them incalculably. Women can aid in the solution of the problem by devoting themselves to Jewish study, by fitting themselves for ordination. The general community can help by showing a willingness to accept women as their spiritual leaders.[4]

Those opposed to ordaining Martha Neumark were afraid that the ordination of women might threaten the authority of Reform rabbis as a whole. They did not believe that there was any need for making such a "radical departure" from Jewish tradition. Neither did they believe that women would raise the standards of the rabbinate. Dr. Jacob Z. Lauterbach summarized their position:

> Nay, all things being equal, women could not even rise to the high standard reached by men in this particular calling. If there is any calling which requires a wholehearted devotion to the exclusion of all other things and the determination to make it one's whole life work, it is the rabbinate. It is not to be considered merely as a livelihood. Nor is it to be entered upon as a temporary occupation. . . . One must choose it for his life work and be prepared to give to it all his energies and to devote to it all the years of his life, constantly learning and improving and thus growing in it. It has been rightly said that the woman who enters a profession, must make her choice between following her chosen profession or the calling of mother and homemaker. She cannot do both well at the same time. This certainly would hold true in the case of the rabbinical profession. The woman who naturally and rightly looks

forward to the opportunity of meeting the right kind of man, of marrying him and of having children and a home of her own, cannot give to the rabbinate that wholehearted devotion which comes from the determination to make it one's life-work. For in all likelihood she could not continue it as a married woman. For, one holding the rabbinical office must teach by precept and example, and must give an example of Jewish family and home life where all the traditional Jewish virtues are cultivated. The rabbi can do so all the better when he is married and has a home and a family of his own. The wife whom God has made as a helpmate to him can be, and in most cases is, of great assistance to him in making his home a Jewish home, a model for the congregation to follow.

In this most important activity of the rabbi, exercising a wholesome influence upon the congregation, the woman rabbi would be deficient. The woman in the rabbinical office could not expect the man to whom she is married to be merely a helpmate to her, assisting her in her rabbinical activities. And even if she could find such a man, willing to take a subordinate position in the family, the influence upon the families in the congregation of such an arrangement in the home and in the family life of the rabbi would not be very wholesome. Not to mention the fact that if she is to be a mother she could not go on with her regular activities in the congregation.

And there is, to my mind, no injustice done to woman by excluding her from this office. There are many avenues open to her if she chooses to do religious or educational work. I can see no reason why we should make this radical departure from traditional practice except the specious argument that we are modern men and, as such, we recognize the full equality of women to men, hence we should be thoroughly consistent. But I would not class the rabbis with those people whose main characteristic is consistency.[5]

Professor David Neumark, father of Martha Neumark, disagreed with his distinguished colleague:

As to the practical question of the advisability to ordain women at the Hebrew Union College, I do not believe that the Orthodox will have any additional reason to object. They themselves employ women in their schools as teachers and readers, and more than this our woman rabbi will not do. In fact the entire question reduces itself to this: Women are already doing most of the work that the ordained woman rabbi is expected to do. But they do it without preparation and without authority. I consider it rather a duty of the authorities to put an end to the prevailing anarchy by giving women a chance to acquire adequate education and an authoritative standing in all branches of religious work. The practical difficulties cannot be denied. But they will work out the same way as in other professions, especially in the teaching profession, from the kindergarten to postgraduate schools. Lydia Rabinowitz raised a family of three children and kept up a full measure of family life while being a professor of bacteriology. The woman rabbi who will remain single will not be more, in fact less, of a problem than the bachelor rabbi. If she marries and chooses to remain a rabbi, and God blesses her, she will retire for a few months and provide a substitute, as rabbis generally do when they are sick or meet with an automobile accident. When she comes back, she will be a better rabbi for the experience. The rabbinate may help the women, and the woman rabbi may help the rabbinate. You cannot treat the Reform rabbinate from the Orthodox point of view. Orthodoxy is orthodoxy and reform is reform. Our good relations with our Orthodox brethren may still be improved by a clear and decided stand on this question. They want us either to be reform or to return to the fold of real genuine Orthodox Judaism whence we came.[6]

Despite the tremendous amount of controversy and discussion that took place in the 1920s and the handful of women who subsequently pursued the rabbinic course of study, the Hebrew Union College-Jewish Institute of Religion did not ordain a woman until 1972 when I be-

came a rabbi. I was not truly the first woman rabbi, however:

> Regina Jonas finished her theological studies at the
> Berlin Academy for the Science of Judaism in the
> middle 1930s. Her thesis subject was: "Can a Woman
> Become a Rabbi?" Of course she set out to prove the
> affirmative.
>
> The faculty accepted her dissertation, but the profes-
> sor of Talmud, the licensing authority, refused to
> ordain her.
>
> The Rev. Max Dieneman, of Offenbach, however, did
> ordain her, and she practiced till 1940, primarily in
> homes for the elderly.
>
> The Germans then dispatched her to the Theresien-
> stadt Concentration Camp where she died of natural
> causes or was sent to the gas chambers.[7]

I was actually the second woman rabbi, then, although I
was the first to be ordained by a theological seminary.

CHAPTER SIX

Economic and Cultural Contributions

As we have seen, man's realm was the synagogue and woman's realm was the home. It was as much a religious responsibility for a woman to raise a family and manage a household as it was for a man to pray three times a day. To maintain a Jewish home, the wife had to pay strict attention to the laws of *kashrut* (dietary laws). She had to develop an atmosphere that was suitable for the transmission of tradition. Her daughters needed an example from which to learn for they too would one day be mothers. Her sons needed to acquire a love for Torah. Her husband needed time to study. All these she was expected to provide and she did through her very able management of family affairs. While her husband was considered the boss it was she who really ran the household. This characterization of the Jewish woman reached its fullest expression during the period of the *shtetl,* the small Jewish village of Eastern Europe.

THE SHTETL WOMAN

One of the *shtetl* woman's primary concerns was education. Her sons would not attend *heder* (Hebrew school) until they were three years old. During their first years, then, they had to be introduced to the concept of education at home. Their mother tried to implant within them a desire to study and created an atmosphere in which learning might flourish. She tried to prepare them for the day when they would spend hours listening to the *melamed* (teacher), learning the letters of the alphabet and struggling with Hebrew texts, so that they would be able to sit beside their fathers in the House of Study and discuss the fine points of Torah and Talmud.

The girls in the family received a minimal education in comparison with their brothers, for study would never be their principal occupation. Their lessons were much shorter because they had to be free to help their mothers at home and to care for younger brothers and sisters. They learned a little Hebrew, enough to be able to recite basic prayers, but seldom enough to understand what they read, and concentrated mostly on Yiddish, so that they could write a letter when necessary and enjoy the vast Yiddish literature that was written primarily for their benefit.

Some girls received a better education than others. If there were no sons in the family, fathers often tried to compensate by turning their daughters into scholars. And in wealthy families the girls sometimes listened as private tutors taught their brothers. They also were more likely to become well versed in the arts. Since they did not have to spend all their time studying Torah, as their brothers did, they were able to enjoy music and languages. Mothers made certain, however, that their daughters did not receive *too* much education. That was unfeminine. All they really had to know was how to manage a household. The more skill they had in this area, the more time their future husbands would have to study and the better off their family would be.

Mark Zborowski and Elizabeth Herzog have described for us the *shtetl* woman:

The ideal woman, commanding as little of the traditional learning as is compatible with reading of her prayers, still contributes to fulfilling the *mitzvah* of learning and all its corollaries. Without her the husband cannot fulfill his obligations and therefore cannot be a good Jew. As a bribe she may bring him dowry and parent-in-law support that enable him to pursue his studies. As a wife she may earn the livelihood while he fulfills "his" *mitzvah*. . . .

The good wife and mother helps her husband to fulfill his obligations. She is responsible for the observance of the dietary laws and for maintaining or implementing all the domestic ritual. Even when her husband performs the ceremony, it is her duty to have in readiness the cup of wine, the loaf of bread, the knife, the towel, the incense, or whatever is needed. She is not included in religious ritual outside of the house, and in fact is not expected to be familiar with it. Moreover, she does not have powers of discretion even in household ceremonials. On any problem of observance she must consult a man—her husband, the rabbi, a respected scholar—and even if she knows the answer by experience she has not the right to decide for herself.

The formal demands upon women are revealed repeatedly in comments on womanly virtue. "She was a perfect Jewish woman, clean, patient, hard-working and silent, submissive to God and to her husband, devoted to her children . . . her own well-being was unimportant. . . . I don't remember my mother sitting at the table when we ate, except for Friday night and Saturdays. Those days she even sat on the whole chair. Other times, when she was sitting, it was always on the edge of the chair. I believe she never ate a whole meal, always some leftovers. When I was older I asked her why she was like that and she said, 'Friday night, on Sabbath Eve, I am a queen, like every Jewish woman. On weekdays I am just a woman . . . !' "

The woman's informal status is more demanding and more rewarding than that formally assigned to her, for in actual living the complementary character of her role is always to the fore. She is the wife, who orders the functioning of the household and provides the setting in which each member performs his part. She is the mother, key figure in the family constellation. Moreover, the more completely her husband fulfills the ideal picture of the man as scholar, the more essential is the wife as realist and mediator between his ivory tower and the hurly-burly of everyday life.[1]

The woman managed the financial affairs of the family. Indeed, in addition to running her household, she generally supported the family through her occupation. She had complete freedom in the marketplace. She did the buying and the selling and knew how to converse with the merchants in the language of the community. While her husband made decisions with regard to domestic ritual, her opinion was decisive when it came to the outside world.

Generally speaking, the roles of men and women in the *shtetl* were accepted without complaint. Men were content to study and women knew that while they respected their husbands as bosses the real power was theirs:

> The *shtetl* is used to the arrangement and besides most people are too busy to give it much thought. "What could a man do without a woman?" is more than a popular saying, it is a constant theme. And how could women get on without men? Besides, this is the way it is and *shtetl* folk are used to accepting a status quo that they might not have recommended had they been consulted in the first place. Certainly few men would want to change places with a busy housewife, cooking, cleaning and perhaps supporting her family by running a small shop. On the other hand, probably few women would care to assume the duties and responsibilities of a *talmid hochem* [learned man] with his countless rituals, his endless study, his incessant discussions and arguments over remote and intricate subjects, his constant anxiety lest he neglect some regulation.
>
> To a large extent, the formal status is dismissed as merely formal. Yes, the women will say, men think we don't count but they're stupid—what could they do

without us? Could they get married? Could they bear children? Could they even be fed and clothed and housed decently? . . .

The pattern prescribed by the culture, however, allows full scope for the "never-silent bell" to be a submissive partner or a vibrant force in her home and the community. A woman may comply with all the formal demands upon her and still be an effective manager of her domestic affairs, an effective businesswoman and an active member of the community. There is room for matriarchs as well as for patriarchs and it would be hard to say which predominate numerically. "My grandmother was a wonderful woman. . . . When we walked down the streets someone would always say, 'There goes Grandmother Leya's grandchild.' . . . My grandfather Yoysef, well, he didn't count for very much."

The wife of a *nogid* [wealthy man] may keep her own private drawer full of trinkets and small cash, from which to help the needy, and it may be to her rather than to him that people turn for help and advice. "She was always busy . . . her good deeds took up so much time." It is not unknown for a man to beg his wife on her deathbed to transfer to him half her *mitzvot,* on the plea that after all they were accomplished with his aid.

To a comfortable degree, in the day-by-day rush of life, each sex is oriented to its own reality. If one's world revolves around the activities of the *shul* [synagogue], the domestic economy is seen as an indispensible but secondary adjunct. If the home is the hub of the universe, the *shul* and its activities become a necessary luxury, sometimes classed as a burden and sometimes as a privilege. In either case, one can feel—mine is the real work of the world.[2]

POINT OF VIEW

The world of the *shtetl* lent itself to the development of distinctive roles for men and women, but modern society is very different. One of the greatest contributions of the feminist movement has been the realization that men and women share equally the responsibility of home and family and the right to pursue a career if they so desire. If future generations are to grow up without the prejudices of their ancestors, then male and female roles as we know them must be expanded and we must provide new role models for our children. Our sons and daughters need to see fathers cooking in the kitchen and mothers active in the world of business. Boys must understand the importance of participating in home life; girls should be encouraged to strive for financial independence. There is no need for one parent to be boss over the other. Both should contribute to the upbringing of children even as both are entitled to engage in interests outside the home.   ෴

ORGANIZATIONAL AFFILIATIONS

Following the mass immigration of Eastern European Jews to the United States at the end of the nineteenth century, the world of the *shtetl* ceased to exist. In the new country men gave up studying and went to work in sweatshops. Women also worked, but only until their husbands could afford to support the family. Then the women were relegated to the home and deprived of the opportunity to make an economic contribution. They had to find fulfillment elsewhere and so they turned to organizational work.

Barred from an active role in worship, women established sisterhoods as a means of participation in the life of the synagogue. The basic task of a sisterhood is to serve the needs of the congregation. More often than not, the sisterhood finances the building of a chapel or the purchase of an organ or the remodeling of the kitchen. The women provide funds for adult education projects, lecture institutes, and study groups. They often maintain the religious school, sometimes paying teachers' salaries and furnishing school supplies. As "room mothers," they provide the necessary

trimmings for the proper celebration of the holidays—
food for the model Seder, candles for Hanukkah, *hamantaschen* (special cakes) for Purim, honey and apples for
Rosh Hashanah.

While the sisterhood's main goal is service to the
synagogue, community projects are not ignored. For example, one of the most prominent and significant projects
sponsored by the National Federation of Temple Sisterhoods is its service to the blind. Sisterhood members spend
many hours a week recording material for the sightless.
With the assistance of Rabbi Michael Aaronsohn, who was
blinded in World War I, this national Reform organization
helped to create the Jewish Braille Institute of America.
Through the Institute, possibly largely through sisterhood
activity and support, the *Jewish Braille Review* is published and made available free of charge to both Jewish
and non-Jewish blind persons.

In addition to sisterhoods, other women's groups
were organized. The first of these was the National Council
of Jewish Women, founded in 1893 by Hannah G. Solomon.
Its original purpose was to further the cause of religious
education and philanthropy, but it soon became active in all
causes that affect humanity. Social reform and human
betterment became its guiding principles.

The history of the National Council of Jewish Women
is closely connected with the history of the United States.
For example, with the dawn of the twentieth century
serious problems developed as a result of increased Jewish
immigration, and the government asked the Council to help.
The Council responded with the development of the Port
and Dock Department, which helped to decrease the threat
of white slavery, exploitation, and sweatshop labor that
faced penniless immigrant women. Council members met all
incoming boats and cared for the immigrants—clothing
them, feeding them, and helping them to find relatives.

By 1911, the Council had developed a complete program in the area of social legislation:

> It championed the elimination of child labor and the provision of adequate housing for low-income groups. It concerned itself also with health opportunities, mothers' pensions, slum clearance, food and drug regulations, wage and hour laws for women, purity of the press and movie censorship, uniform marriage and divorce laws, civil service for government employees, and the enactment of Federal anti-lynching laws—in short, all forms of legislation for the protection of children and women.[3]

As World War II approached, the council grappled with the problem of anti-Semitism:

> In order to stimulate interest in Jewish affairs, and to fortify Jewish women with a knowledge of Jewish history, tradition, and culture, so that they might combat the disintegrating forces of anti-Semitism and discrimination, Mrs. Arthur Brin, Mrs. Alexander Kohut, Mrs. Maurice L. Goldman and Mrs. Mary G. Schonberg, Executive Director, met in New York in 1934 and laid plans for the organization of a Committee of One Thousand to assume leadership in these activities. In 1935 this temporary committee was expanded into the Department of Contemporary Jewish Affairs, which also included the work formerly done by the committees on religion and religious education. Its timely and widely distributed pamphlet, "Anti-Semitism: A Study Outline," stimulated 145 sections to develop active study groups on the subject. This pamphlet was one of the earliest attempts by any organization in America to meet logically and intelligently, with frank recognition of its import, this old and vital problem of Western civilization.
> But the National Council of Jewish Women did not content itself with study alone. Just as it had pioneered in the 1890s in study circles and in direct social action, so again during the troubled 1930s it demonstrated

its devotion to faith and humanity by giving prompt aid to Jewish refugee children from Germany. In 1934 it cooperated with other organizations and public-spirited citizens in forming the German Jewish Children's Aid, through whose efforts hundreds of Jewish children were rescued from Nazi oppression and placed in private homes in America, to be given the privilege of becoming citizens of the United States when they should reach the age of twenty-one.[4]

In the years that followed, the National Council of Jewish Women continued to help the underprivileged, the refugee, the immigrant, the orphan, the soldier, and all who needed assistance. Women from all branches of Judaism joined together to grapple with the problems that faced their local communities and their nation. They were most concerned with the problems that directly affected the Jewish community but they were also involved in the total community. From the beginning, the passage of social legislation was one of the Council's most basic aims, and social justice remains its most specific goal.

Another basic concern of women's organizations was service to Israel. In 1912, Henrietta Szold was instrumental in organizing Hadassah, the American women's Zionist organization. Hadassah's greatest contribution has been its medical program. Since its inception, Hadassah has met the medical needs of those living in Palestine, battling such diseases as malaria, trachoma, cholera, and tuberculosis. In 1939 the first patients were admitted to the Rothschild–Hadassah-University Hospital on Mt. Scopus, and by 1949 fifty students were enrolled in the Hebrew University–Hadassah Medical School. Today, the Hadassah medical program is highly esteemed among the international medical community: healing, teaching, and research are its basic principles. Hadassah Hospital maintains forty-eight medical departments and clinics; Hadassah doctors travel around the world helping young countries establish medical services;

Hadassah scientists publish over four hundred research papers a year. To the deprived and the depressed, Hadassah represents promise and life.

Hadassah supports other programs as well. The *Aliyat HaNoar* was developed in 1934 in answer to the threat of Nazism. It was dedicated to the rescue and transfer of Jewish children from Europe to Palestine. Today over 125,000 Youth Aliyah graduates are making their contributions to the State of Israel in every field from agriculture to industry, from teaching to creative arts, from the defense forces to the diplomatic services. Other key Hadassah projects include its program in the area of vocational education, its support of the Jewish National Fund, its volunteer service organization called *Ya'al,* and its concern with Jewish education.

In America, Hadassah's aim is the furthering of democratic ideals and the spread of knowledge and understanding. Official positions are issued in matters of significance which face the nation. Hadassah leaders are invited to attend briefing sessions sponsored by the government, and its members are kept informed on current issues. Representatives participate in local and national conferences, and *Hadassah* magazine, with one of the broadest circulations of all Jewish periodicals, exerts a weighty influence on the general Jewish community.

Another organization which emphasizes commitment to Israel is Pioneer Women. Founded in 1925, it is the American branch of Israel's *Moetzet Hapoalot* political party, founded four years earlier. Its aim is to train and educate the Israeli woman and her family so that they can live productive lives, and its task is to provide the necessary social service and educational assistance to achieve this goal.

Much of Pioneer Women's work is concerned with children. It was the first organization to establish day-care centers and kindergartens for children of working mothers. It maintains homes for orphans and summer camps for young people from culturally deprived homes. Group work is carried out with adolescent girls who are having difficulty coping with the problems of emerging womanhood. After-school clubs have been established for those who need a place to study.

From its inception, Pioneer Women has been concerned with the rebuilding of the land. As a result, four agricultural schools are operated to provide training for those interested in the rural development of Israel. Both academic studies and courses in agriculture are taught, and practical experience is gained through work on farms, orchards, plant nurseries, granaries, and the like.

Another area of concern is vocational training, where the primary goal of Pioneer Women has been to teach people to develop skills that will make them economically independent. Over four hundred vocational schools and courses are operated in cooperation with government agencies, and there is a special emphasis on group work with Arab and Druze women living in Israel. In all its programs, Pioneer Women emphasizes the importance of human dignity.

Another organization that is primarily concerned with vocational training is the Organization for Rehabilitation through Training (ORT). It began in 1880 in Russia when a small group of men joined together to provide loans for Jewish artisans who wanted to buy tools and equipment. As the years passed, trade schools, workshops, and apprenticeships were made available to those who wanted to learn, and every effort was made to improve the quality of Jewish labor. By 1921 an international organization was formed and training programs were established throughout the world.

Women's American ORT was founded in 1927. Its membership grew quickly and today ORT chapters are functioning in every major community in the United States. Women have made significant contributions, particularly in the area of fund raising, and have financed the training of teachers, medical services for students, social service assistance for food, clothing, and recreation, apprenticeship and advanced adult training programs, and school construction. Indeed, ORT has become the largest privately financed vocational training school system in the world.

Some women's organizations were established as auxiliaries to men's organizations. One such is B'nai B'rith Women. B'nai B'rith, the oldest Jewish service organization in America, was founded in 1843. It has always been concerned with the welfare and survival of the Jewish people as well as the progress of humanity, and has traditionally been in the forefront of the struggle for justice and equality.

When it was established, B'nai B'rith was strictly a male organization. Beginning in 1859, however, proposals were periodically made and rejected that women be accepted as members. Finally in 1895 the formation of women's auxiliaries was permitted. For many years these auxiliaries were few in number, but by 1930 they had begun to grow rapidly. Women wanted to participate fully in the activities of the organization and in 1938 they sought representation at the Supreme Lodge conventions. They did not receive it.

For the next triennial convention each women's district was permitted one representative with voice but no vote, and she was to attend at her own district's expense. But these women wanted to be more active and so in 1940 the presidents of the six women's districts formed the B'nai B'rith Women's Supreme Council. The Council had little influence or power but this kind of national recognition inspired the members to work even harder. Finally in 1950 the women were granted full representation on the order's executive committee and one member from each women's district was given full delegate status at Supreme Lodge conventions. It had taken a long time for women to be given their rightful place in the oldest Jewish service organization.

B'nai B'rith Women now supports numerous projects, among which are Hillel foundations for college youth, the Anti-Defamation League, Operation Stork (in cooperation with the March of Dimes), the B'nai B'rith Youth Organization, the Leo N. Levi National Arthritis Hospital, the B'nai B'rith Center at Rochester, the Franklin Delano Roosevelt Four Freedoms Library in Washington, D.C., and the B'nai B'rith Women Children's Home in Israel for emotionally disturbed youngsters. Like its sister organizations, B'nai B'rith Women has been concerned with the changing status of women in modern society. For example, the platform adopted at the 1974 International Convention contained this statement:

> B'nai B'rith Women, as a supporter of the rights of women as equal participants in our society, is dedicated to the prompt ratification of the Equal Rights Amendment of the U.S. Constitution and we urge such ratification by all the states.
>
> The status of women has steadily improved in recent years. In the majority of countries, women have the right to vote and to participate in the electoral process. They serve, though in proportionately limited numbers, in national parliaments, are members of Congress, legislatures and the judiciary in many countries. In their ranks are ambassadors, diplomats, mayors of cities, members of school boards, civil servants, lawyers, physicians and aquanauts.
>
> Many laws, regulations and practices which once discriminated against women have been repealed or amended. Nevertheless, there are still many serious inequities affecting the status of women under law.
>
> It is imperative that business and industry as well as the professions initiate and implement an open door

policy for entry, placement, recognition and advancement of women. Enlarging opportunities for women to hold political office and to participate equally in appointive posts on public advisory committees and commissions at all levels of government is long overdue. We urge that governments likewise place women in far greater numbers in positions of trust and responsibility.

B'nai B'rith Women advocates that business and industry equate relevant specific volunteer experience in relation to job entry.

High quality and adequate day care facilities for children must be provided through the initiative and support of both public and private sources.

Ratification, enforcement and enactment of U.N. Conventions will eliminate political discrimination as well as discrimination on the basis of sex. Therefore, B'nai B'rith Women advocates continued support of the Commission on the Status of Women and the various national Commissions.

The right of a woman to plan her family through free choice must be guaranteed. Antiquated laws restricting family planning and contraception information, or forbidding abortions should be abolished.

B'nai B'rith Women urges the government of Israel to examine its legislation regarding the rights of widows. We urge the freeing of those women from their deceased husbands' families, giving them the legal right to decide their own marital future.

How women exercise their prerogatives, carry out their responsibilities and work together to attain their full rights and recognition will be the determining factor in attaining their birthright—true and equal status in the world society.[5]

POINT OF VIEW

As this review of women's organizations clearly indicates, Jewish women are concerned with the changing status of women in general. It is interesting to note, however, that the above statement failed to call for equality within the religious community. Every other field of endeavor was mentioned, but these women did not demand an equal role within the synagogue. Until they do, real equality can not be established.

For whatever reasons, women are much more involved in organizational work than men are. They are far more concerned with providing social services to the community. Unfortunately, however, they have been permitted to occupy top leadership positions only in their own organizations, and have not been permitted to bring their talents and skills to community organizations. Jacqueline K. Levine, President of the Women's Division of the American Jewish Congress, put it well when she said:

> Women's communal activism has become so overwhelming that a woman luncheon speaker recently proposed that, rather than calling ourselves professional volunteers, we women might more appropriately be referred to as volunteer professionals. I assent to this suggestion. For, volunteer professionals that we are, we perform a dizzying catalogue of assignments without pay; and—to judge by the number of social experiments which have derived from women's voluntary organizations—most productively. Progressive child education programs, Head Start, the provision of sheltered workshops for handicapped workers, recreation for the aged; *all* were begun by women. Should not the Jewish women volunteers give their expertise and understanding where most needed? At the top. We wish to share, not glory, but responsibility. We wish to offer the independence of our thinking.[6]

Jewish women are to be congratulated for the tremendous contributions they have made through their organizational affiliations. We have improved the quality of life for all humanity. Now the time has come for us to demand equality in all phases of communal work so that we may truly share our knowledge and experience.

3

JEWISH
WOMEN
IN
THE
MODERN
WORLD

CHAPTER SEVEN

The Jewish Mother Stereotype

The Jewish mother stereotype began in biblical times, when a woman's reasons for living were portrayed as marriage and motherhood. So it has been assumed ever since. Even the matriarchs were portrayed as overprotective mothers who would do anything for the benefit of their husbands and children. Throughout the centuries other qualities were added to this characterization of the Jewish woman—her talkativeness, her ability to nag, her constant concern with feeding those around her, and her emphasis on the education and achievement of her children. As a result, the portrayal of the fat, noisy, anxious, bossy Jewish mother finds a welcome place in the pages of modern literature.

MARJORIE MORNINGSTAR

The first major American literary work to portray the struggles of a Jewish girl passing from girlhood to womanhood was *Marjorie Morningstar,* by Herman Wouk. In it, Marjorie is an idealistic and ambitious young woman who insists that she's "going to be an actress, not a fat dull housewife with a big engagement ring." She becomes completely enamored of the world of show business, and her relationship with Noel Airman, a brilliant eligible bachelor who has the reputation of being little more than a "fascinating loafer," adds to her excitement.

Marjorie's desire for a career precipitates tremendous opposition from her mother. Mrs. Morgenstern does not hesitate to express her wish that Marjorie marry a doctor or lawyer and present her parents with grandchildren whom they can enjoy in their latter years. She is a typical Jewish mother, as Noel explains in his description of a typical Jewish girl:

> I dutifully began making the rounds of the West Side among the eligible girls. I must have had dates with nine-tenths of them. That's how I became such a connoisseur of Shirley. I went out with Shirley after Shirley. It was uncanny. She was uncanny. She was everywhere. I would hear about some wonderful new girl—Susan Fain, Helen Kaplan, Judy Morris, the name didn't matter. I'd telephone her, make a date, go up to the apartment, she'd open the door—and there would stand Shirley. In a different dress, a different body, looking at me out of different eyes, but with that one unchanging look, the look of Shirley. The respectable girl, the mother of the next generation, all tricked out to appear gay and girlish and carefree, but with a terrible threatening solid dullness jutting through, like the gray rocks under the spring grass in Central Park. Behind her, half the time, would loom her mother, the frightful giveaway, with the same face as Helen's or Susan's, only coarsened, wrinkled, fattened, with the deceiving bloom of girlhood all stripped away, showing naked the grim horrid respectable determined *dullness,* oh God. . . . Oh, God, Marjorie, the dullness of the mothers! Smug self-righteousness mixed with climbing eagerness, and a district attorney's inquisitive suspicion—*Judge Erhmann's oldest boy, they say he's brilliant but I don't know, not solid, wants to be a composer, something crazy like that, also I hear he's been mixed up with women, doesn't do his work at school*—Marjorie, it's amazing, absolutely amazing, how the grapevine works among the mothers. I was feared. The

word was out that I was a fascinating loafer. It was quite true. The peculiar thing was that I affected Shirley the way whiskey hits an Indian. She knew I was bad for her, but I drove her crazy. Marjorie, I have my conceit, but it doesn't extend to my romantic career on the West Side. I tell you soberly I was like a man with a cane walking down a lane of hyacinths, smashing flowers right and left. They all recovered, mind you. Shirley is indestructible. They're all married now—to dentists, doctors, woolen manufacturers, lawyers, whatever you please—but I assure you they remember Saul Ehrmann. And it wasn't always one-sided. I remember a couple of them. I've been ragingly in love with Shirley, you see. That's the worst tormentor of all.[1]

Noel continues his tirade with a description of "Shirley's" hypocrisy:

Shirley doesn't play fair, you see. What she wants is what a woman should want, always has and always will—big diamond ring, house in a good neighborhood, furniture, children, well-made clothes, furs—but she'll never say so. Because in our time those things are supposed to be stuffy and dull. She knows that. She reads novels. So, half believing what she says, she'll tell you the hell with that domestic dullness, never for her. She's going to paint, that's what—or be a social worker, or a psychiatrist, or an interior decorator, or an actress, always an actress if she's got any real looks—but the idea is she's going to *be* somebody. Not just a wife. Perish the thought![2]

Marjorie is determined not to be another Shirley. She even loses her virginity. But in the end she betrays herself and joins the ranks of the stereotyped Jewish mother by becoming Mrs. Milton Schwartz. That she chooses to become a housewife rather than pursue a career in acting reflects the attitude that marriage is not only a necessity for a woman but the only thing she really wants.

And in Marjorie's case, as the critic Leslie Fiedler has suggested, the full enjoyment of her marriage is marred by her loss of virginity and she is in some way permanently maimed although Wouk has insisted on a bittersweet happy ending.[3]

POINT OF VIEW

Once again the stereotyped image of the Jewish mother has triumphed and there is no recognition of the fact that a woman might desire something more than just a husband and children, that she might need to fulfill her creative potential in some way other than running a household. We are still waiting for a literary work which will portray the inner conflicts and outer obstacles with which a Jewish woman must contend as she seeks to fulfill her potential in whatever way she finds meaningful, be it marriage or career or both. ❧

MRS. PORTNOY

A most popular characterization of the Jewish mother may be found in *Portnoy's Complaint* by Philip Roth. It is also unfair. As Marie Syrkin explains:

> Sophie, the mother, is not even a plausible type, let alone an individual. She is a synthetic production, an amalgam of clichés, with touches from the orthodox *shtetl* alternating with bits from middle-class suburbia. Mamma veers from a fixation on orthodox ritual, perhaps true of her mother, to a lack of decorum in her intimate behavior in the presence of her son which would be a travesty of grandma. Roth manages to endow the lady with both earlier taboos and later license, so offering the worst of both worlds. A collection of gags . . . Sophie . . . becomes a grotesque festooned with dirty toilet paper, the whole held together by a thick glue of elementary as well as alimentary

Freud. Roth's chief contribution to the Jewish mother routine is the picture of momma threatening her son with a long bread knife to make him eat. To make sure that this maniacal bit is viewed as characteristic of the type rather than as an individual aberration, the Jewish ladies who come to play Mah-Jongg applaud this technique in child care.[4]

Portnoy's complaint is that his mother's love for him is too overpowering, that she never lets him alone. Bruno Bettelheim suggests, however, that Portnoy possesses an overpowering love for his mother which is then turned into a negative projection. Whatever his mother does for him is not enough; he always wants more. Like the stereotyped Jewish mother, she is not permitted to have a life of her own; everything she does must revolve around her son. Only then will Portnoy be satisfied. In the meantime he blames all failure on his mother. As Bettelheim explains:

> The long-suffering Jewish mother who suffers herself to be blamed for everything, is willing to thus serve her son. Never will he have to feel guilty about anything he does because he can always blame it on her. And in a way he can; but not as he thinks. He can blame her for what she has led him to believe: That whatever he wants he must immediately be given. This, the central theme of his life, he screams out at the *kibbutz* girl: "I HAVE TO HAVE." It is she who finally tells him that this belief of his—that he has to have what he wants, whatever it may cost the other—is not valid.
> In a fantasy of being judged for his crimes, he realizes, at least for a moment, that blaming his mother will not get him off, cannot justify his behavior to others.[5]

Portnoy feels that his mother has enslaved him when in reality he has enslaved himself to her. Through his numerous sexual encounters with non-Jewish girls, he is actually remaining faithful to his mother as well as keeping from his parents what they want so much—grandchildren.

Although Roth's characters are certainly Jewish stereotypes, their characteristics are not found only among Jews. As Rabbi Arthur Lelyveld suggests,

> the overprotective, overloving and overdemanding mother, as well as the *schlimazeldiker* and *nebichdiker* failure of a father, are not necessarily Jewish types, even though they are Jewish stereotypes. Popular wisdom tells us that. "You don't have to be Jewish to be a Jewish mother." As I read the book, I reflected frequently on the thought that among that segment of the adult population that is sick, there are undoubtedly a proportionate number of sick people who were warped by Gentile fathers who were *schlemiels,* or by matriarchal Gentile mothers. Oedipus and Electra [the classic literary types] were not Jewish.[6]

POINT OF VIEW

More often than not, fiction reflects views commonly held by society. If women are to be free and equal, then we must overcome the fixed images people have of others and move away from stereotyped thinking. Perhaps the best way to conquer ignorance and fear is to embark upon an intensive program of education. When enough people learn that numerous Jewish women have made significant contributions to humanity, above and beyond family life, then the stereotyped image of the Jewish mother will be revised, and ultimately we will reject feminine stereotypes of any kind.

POSITIVE ASPECTS

Thus far, we have considered only negative portrayals of the Jewish mother stereotype. What about its positive aspects? Hasn't the modern Jewish woman turned what many have always considered liabilities into valuable assets?

For example, we all know that a Jewish mother is very talkative, that she hardly ever lets you get a word in edgewise. But Zena Smith Blau suggests that this is an admirable quality.

> Another stimulus to intellectual aptitude was the talkativeness of the Jewish home. It is now recognized that exposure to this factor in their early formative years increases the learning readiness of children, and it has long been known that verbal skill is an important component of I.Q. and achievement test performance. That Yiddishe Mamehs, in particular, were talkative, any Jewish male will ruefully confirm, but it is not generally recognized that this notorious attribute of theirs gave their children a head start in learning. Whatever Yiddishe Mamehs did for their children—and they did a great deal—was accompanied by a flow of language, consisting of rich, colorful, expressive words and phrases. Their vocabulary of endearments alone could fill a modest sized paperback, but they also had a superb store of admonishments, curses, imprecations, explanations, songs and folksayings that they effortlessly invoked as they went about ministering to the needs of their children and their husbands. The freedom that they exhibited with the spoken word invited a similar response from their children and it carried over into school despite the fact that Yiddish, and not English, was their mother tongue. This helps account for the fact that learning aptitude was demonstrated not only by Jewish children whose fathers had extensive religious learning but also by those from homes where learning and cultivation were largely absent.[7]

Jewish mothers have always placed a special emphasis on the education and achievement of their children. They would make any sacrifice to have a doctor, lawyer, or accountant in the family.

> Jewish immigrants were no better off economically when they settled in America than other immigrants; they lived in the same squalid neighborhoods; their

children attended the same schools and learned from the same teachers but, as a rule, they exhibited a greater aptitude for learning and a greater will to learn than non-Jewish children. Learning, of course, has traditionally commanded respect even among the Jewish masses who, as a rule, had only a meager amount of secular or religious education. Every indication of intellectual curiosity and verbal precocity in their children was received with pleasure and delight by Jewish parents, and long before their formal schooling began Jewish youngsters understood that there was no more effective way to win approval and praise from adults. Even an impudent question or a naughty remark, if clever, was received with amused tolerance by parents and proudly relayed to friends and relatives as evidence of *hochma,* which is the Hebrew word for wisdom, but also is used colloquially to denote brightness, cleverness or wit.[8]

We all know that a Jewish mother detests an empty mouth. She will do everything in her power to keep your plate full and your stomach stuffed.

Teaching of the basic precepts of Judaism began virtually in infancy for Jewish children whether they were brought up in religious or in secular homes. The kind of appeal that Yiddishe Mamehs employed to motivate their children to eat, for example, was often couched in normative terms. They didn't simply impress on their children that eating was an act of self-interest—that by doing so they would grow up big and strong—but they also invested this mundane activity with moral significance and transformed it into an act of altruism by urging the child to eat for *others*—for mama, for poppa, for other members of the family, and inevitably, the appeal was made to eat for "the poor, starving children in Europe." [9]

No one possesses a capacity for nagging quite like the Jewish mother. Before you know it, you're agreeing with her just to keep her quiet!

Yiddishe Mamehs seemed singularly unconcerned with "discipline" and "independence training." They allowed their children a greater degree of liberty at home than was customary among Gentiles, and readily acknowledged that their children were *zelosen,* that is, pampered, demanding, spoiled, not well behaved the way Gentile children seemed to be in the presence of their mothers. The Anglo-Saxon code of stoic endurance and suppressed emotion was alien to the Eastern European Jew. Of course, Yiddishe Mamehs had their boiling point, which varied a good deal depending on their individual temperament, but generally they preferred controlling their children *mit guten,* that is, by explanation, reasoning, distraction, and admonishment. As a rule, they were naggers or screamers rather than disciplinarians. They gained compliance by entreaties repeated so often that finally the child would comply voluntarily, albeit wearily, to their requests. The Yiddishe Mameh avoided fear of herself in the child, and regarded such methods as morally wrong as well as inexpedient for cultivating inner controls in her children.[10]

A Jewish mother just would not be a Jewish mother without being overprotective. She hovers over her children, attempting to shelter them from disappointment and sometimes from reality itself.

The determined struggle of Jewish mothers to delay the emotional emancipation of their children is well known and often criticized but it was nevertheless a significant factor in the high educational attainment of second generation Jews in America. It is to their credit, I think, that they recognized that the basic conditions required to fashion a talmudic scholar are very much the same as those needed to achieve any other career requiring a high order of intellectual skill. In both cases, a prolonged period of time and arduous work must be spent in acquiring a complex body of knowledge, during which time the child must be provided encouragement and emotional support as well as protection from outside influence which might lure him into abandoning long-run plans for more immediate pleasures and rewards. Yiddishe Mamehs achieved this by denying the legitimacy of their children's declarations of independence. *Mainst as du bist shoin a ganzer mensch* (You only think you are a responsible human being) was their stock retort to youthful emancipation proclamations. They employed every stratagem to remain as indispensable to their children in later childhood and adolescence as they had been in earlier life. The concept of early independence training was foreign to their thinking. According to their view a child was a child whether he was five or fifteen and required much the same order of care, devotion and protection in adolescence as in childhood. With respect to learning and intellectual matters generally they encouraged the development of self-reliance and autonomy, but they were reluctant to grant their children other forms of independence or to impose any serious responsibility on them until they had completed their education and were ready to assume the obligations of marriage and a career.[11]

For centuries, Jewish mothers have been blamed for their children's psychological and emotional problems. Isn't it about time that we recognize the tremendous contributions they have made which have led to the remarkable intellectual achievements of their children?

POINT OF VIEW

The Jewish mother stereotype developed out of a society in which women had only one option : that of wife and mother. For many, it remains a viable role model and should not be abolished. In fact, true liberation means accepting homemaking as dignified work rather than degrading it as inferior. It is grossly unfair to deprive women of the satisfaction so many of them experience as wives and mothers. The creative skill which housewifery and motherhood require should be recognized and praised.

At the same time we must realize that modern society demands more than the sole option of being a wife and mother. For one thing, increased life expectancy gives us many more years of creativity than ever before, and we should all be free to choose our own life-style. Those women, whether married or single, who opt for careers will serve as new role models for future generations, and hopefully the day will come when little girls (and little boys) will know that they can aspire and work toward any goal with a chance of success.

CHAPTER EIGHT

Great Jewish Women

Rebecca Gratz founded the first Sunday School in Philadelphia. Emma Lazarus wrote "The New Colossus," the poem inscribed on the Statute of Liberty. The German Jewess Gluckel of Hameln wrote her memoirs, an unusual and unique means of self-expression for a woman and a work that provides invaluable insight into the life of the Jews in Central Europe in the seventeenth century. Dona Gracia Mendes struggled to maintain her Jewish identity during the Spanish Inquisition. Emma Goldman was a leading feminist and pioneer advocate of birth control, an anarchist lecturer and agitator for free speech. The Henry Street Settlement in New York City was founded by a pioneer social worker named Lillian Wald. Nelly Sachs won the Nobel Prize for Literature. The Honorable Lily Montagu made religion the essence of her life and helped to found the Liberal Jewish Movement in England. Trude Weiss-Rosmarin is respected for her scholarly opinions and editorship of *The Jewish Spectator*. These and numerous other Jewish women have long deserved recognition for their accomplishments and achievements, but unfortunately have been practically ignored. You may therefore have never heard of the women about whom you are now going to read—all but one, that is.

ERNESTINE ROSE

Ernestine Rose opposed the traditional role of women from childhood. Born in 1810 in a Polish ghetto, she was the daughter of a rabbi. She preferred reading and studying to sewing and cooking, and she pleaded with her father to give her an education. Finally he relented and engaged a private tutor. At the age of sixteen, she refused to marry the man her father had chosen for her, and she went to court to force her father to return her inheritance to her.

Her career as a social reformer and persuasive crusader also began at an early age. Traveling through Europe, she was shocked to learn that Polish Jews were not welcome in Germany. She decided to complain to the king. The Prussian monarch granted her an audience and she told him face to face that his treatment of the Jews was inhuman and unjust. As a result, the king made an exception and permitted her to remain in Germany for as long as she wanted.

She married William Rose and in 1836 they set sail for America. She was disappointed to find that women in the United States were no better off than women in Europe. They had no legal rights and were not permitted to seek fulfillment outside the home. Ernestine quickly realized that the situation called for more than mere discussion; the time was ripe for agitation. When a resolution was introduced in the New York legislature to protect the rights and property of married women, Ernestine went door-to-door collecting signatures on a petition in support. Her job was not easy. Time and again doors were slammed in her face. In five months of work she was able to get only five signatures. It was twelve years before the bill was passed.

Ernestine viewed the area of women's rights as part

of the larger problem of human rights and she soon involved herself in the fight against slavery. She became a public spokeswoman for the Abolitionist movement. People flocked to hear her, probably because it was such a novelty to hear a woman express opinions on public issues, and she soon became known as the "Queen of the Platform." Her motto was "Agitate! Agitate!" and wherever she went the cry of infidel followed her. She traveled throughout the country and was nearly tarred and feathered when she denounced slavery in Charleston, South Carolina.

The first national women's rights convention was held in Worcester, Massachusetts, in 1850, and Ernestine Rose was the featured speaker. Among others attending were Lucy Stone and Lucretia Mott, William Lloyd Garrison and Frederick Douglas. Ernestine was appointed to the central committee, and she emphasized the need to work for women's rights throughout the world. As can be expected, the press was quite hostile to the women's movement and the clergy even more so. Often ministers would appear at rallies with Bibles in hand to quote scripture as proof that women were inferior to men. Ernestine was quite capable of holding her own, however, and she insisted that women be given rights not as a gift of charity but as an act of justice.

By 1854 the women of New York were planning to converge on the state capital. They had drawn up a list of basic demands.

> 1) A law granting married women the right to own the money and property they earned during their marriage, as well as the right to buy, sell, sign a contract and engage in business activities of their own.
> 2) A law granting mothers the custody of their children. (According to existing laws a father who was in debt and needed money could hire out his children to anybody he wished, without the mother's consent. And

if he wanted to, he could take the children away from their mother altogether and pass them on to a guardian of his own choice.)

3) A law granting women the right to sue and be sued, the right to be tried by a jury and to have women on the jury whenever a woman was on trial.

4) Finally and most importantly, a law granting women the right to vote and be voted for.[1]

Under Susan B. Anthony's direction, thirteen thousand signatures were obtained in favor of these demands, but the convention in Albany accomplished nothing in terms of practical results. Ernestine Rose consoled a disappointed Susan B. Anthony by reminding her that the petitions did have an important effect on the signers even if the legislators appeared unconcerned. For many of these women, signing a petition represented their first step toward freedom.

Yuri Suhl later analyzed the public reaction to the Albany women's convention:

The newspapers focused much of their attention on Ernestine. She was singled out for either high praise or vicious attack. One reporter, describing a meeting at which she spoke, wrote, "But Mrs. Rose is the queen of the company. . . . She has as great a power to chain an audience as any of our best male speakers."

Another newspaper could not see why people should want to listen to such "foreign propagandists as the ringleted, glove-handed, exotic Ernestine Rose" who came to this country because "she was compelled to fly in pursuit of freedom." Busy as she was, Ernestine sat down and dashed off a letter to the editor:

"I left my country not flying but deliberately," she wrote. "I chose to make this country my home in preference to any other, because if you carried out the theories you profess, it would indeed be the noblest country on earth. And as my countrymen so nobly aided in the physical struggle for Freedom and Independence,

I felt, and still feel it equally my duty to use my humble abilities to the uttermost in my power to aid in the great moral struggle for human rights and human freedom." [2]

Her health began to fail, but Ernestine continued to travel throughout the country in behalf of equal rights for all. As the fifth national women's rights convention approached, a conflict surrounding Ernestine arose. Some wanted her to be president of the convention; others thought her too controversial and were afraid that her presence as president would invite attacks upon the movement as a whole. But Susan B. Anthony believed that Ernestine deserved the presidency and at last the majority agreed. When the convention was over, a resolution was passed unanimously thanking Ernestine for the manner in which she had conducted the proceedings.

The struggle continued and by 1860 women had received everything they had demanded except the right to vote. They approached the tenth annual convention with enthusiasm and excitement. Little did they know that suffrage was still so far away. At that convention, Ernestine congratulated them and urged them to persist in their efforts: "Freedom, my friends, does not come from the clouds, like a meteor; it does not bloom in one night; it does not come without great efforts and great sacrifices; all who love liberty have to labor for it."

Then came the Civil War, and the next convention was not held until the spring of 1863. Delegates came primarily to discuss ways in which they could aid the government. It became clear in the years that followed that there would be a split in the fight for the rights of the Negro and the rights of women. Women felt betrayed. The Fourteenth and Fifteenth Amendments ignored them. The Abolitionist leaders had turned their backs on the struggle for women's rights; they were concerned only with the Negro. The rift grew wider between the equal-rights and anti-slavery advocates and by 1869 the Equal Rights Association became the National Woman's Suffrage Association. By this time, however, Ernestine's health was so poor that she was forced to curtail her activities. Her remaining years were spent in England.

As she fought for women's rights and for the liberation of the slave, Ernestine also found time to defend the Jewish people. When she discovered an anti-Semitic editorial in the *Boston Investigator,* she immediately wrote to Horace Seaver, the editor:

> I almost smelt brimstone, genuine Christian brimstone, when I read in the *Investigator*—"Even the modern Jews are bigoted, narrow, exclusive, and totally unfit for progressive people like the Americans among whom we hope they may not spread." Indeed! You "hope." Now suppose you had the power. . . . Would you drive them out of Boston—out of progressive America as they were once driven out of Spain? . . .
>
> The nature of the Jew is governed by the same laws as human nature in general . . . let the subject be impartially investigated and it will be found that take them all in all the Jews are as good as any other sect. . . . Will you tell me they are cunning, sharp traders? Then I will point out to you the renowned "Yankee" who, it is admitted by all, excels the Jew in that art. . . . Do not add to the prejudice already existing toward the Jews, or any other sect.[3]

The editor printed Ernestine's letter but added an anti-Semitic reply which she could not let go unanswered. For nearly three months their correspondence continued and if nothing else the readers of the *Boston Investigator* at least gained a basic knowledge of Jews and Jewish history.

Years later this same editor wrote an editorial about Ernestine. Yuri Suhl explains:

His letter was a reply to the *Revolution* where, in the summer of 1870, he read the following statement: "First of all there is Lucretia Mott . . . then Elizabeth Cady Stanton . . . then Pauline Wright Davis . . . then Lucy Stone . . . then Susan B. Anthony . . . then, later, Anna E. Dickinson . . . noble, cultivated gifted women, who are now apprenticing their best energies to the enfranchisement of their sex." Incredible! the editor thought, only one year away from home and already forgotten! And so he wrote an editorial entitled "Mrs. Ernestine L. Rose" in which he said, "To omit her name from the catalogue is like playing Hamlet with the character of Hamlet left out. . . . These are all able women, but not one of them has done any more for the cause of woman than Ernestine L. Rose, if indeed as much." [4]

BERTHA PAPPENHEIM

At the end of the nineteenth century the Jews were forced to flee the pogroms of Eastern Europe. Many of the refugees sought shelter in Frankfurt, Germany, where a welfare center was established by a group of Jewish women to care for them. The sight of these homeless and hungry people, old and tired or young and frail, standing in line for a bowl of warm soup, had a profound effect on one of the volunteers, twenty-nine-year-old Bertha Pappenheim.

She could have lived, if she wished, like her mother, in quiet leisure, with money enough for endless entertainment and travel. But something within her cried out for a life that held deeper meaning.

She did not know how to seek this kind of life however until the day she stood in the soup kitchen, surrounded by the persecuted men, women, and children. She felt she must help these stricken souls. It was her responsibility as a Jew, as a woman, as a human being.

She knew it as a certainty the moment she asked the little girl with the brown eyes where she would live and the child had replied, "I don't know," with fear in her eyes.

The little girl's eyes haunted her. A child should not have to know such fear—a child should have a mother and father to take care of him, and if a child lost his mother and father because of the barbaric cruelty of man toward man, others must accept responsibility for the child so he could live without fear.[5]

Bertha Pappenheim's most immediate response to her experience in the soup kitchen was to begin volunteering her time at the Girls' Orphanage, an institution supported primarily by Jewish women for the purpose of caring for baby girls who were orphans or whose parents were unable to support them or who were illegitimate and unwanted. When the director of the Orphanage became ill, Bertha was appointed the new administrator.

She looked beyond the years that the girls would spend in the orphanage. She wanted to prepare them for life in the outside world, to teach them to learn and to think, to experience all the joys that life had to offer. Therefore, in addition to teaching the girls household management, she started kindergarten classes for the little girls and classes in history, geography, art appreciation, and music for the older ones. She felt responsible for their future, and she made every effort to give them the tools they would need to cope with the world.

Bertha firmly believed that women had a right to a higher education, and she resented the fact that she had been deprived of one. It was ridiculous to assume that a girl of sixteen should stop thinking and studying and instead spend all her time waiting for some man to marry her so she could spend her entire life running a house and raising a family. Bertha believed in women's rights. She became an ardent feminist. She translated Mary Wollstonecraft's *A Vindication of the Rights of Women* from English into German and wrote a play of her own in which she emphasized certain inequalities in Jewish civil law. She was convinced that education was a necessity. Only educated women would cease to consider themselves inferior to men.

Bertha was also an organizer, and when she discovered that Jewish welfare work lacked a systematic structure, she turned her talents to the task of giving it one. She founded a local organization called Care by Women and personally taught its members social-work techniques. She appointed committees to establish nursery schools, find foster homes for unwanted children, and provide much-needed career and family counseling for women. She emphasized the need for national unity among Jewish women, and in 1904 founded the Federation of Jewish Women and became its first president. Its purpose was to support orphanages and hospitals as well as to provide training for nurses and social workers. She was "responsible for the welding of the feminist philosophy with the philanthropic spirit."

Another area that particularly concerned Bertha was the white-slave market. The incredible poverty that existed in the ghettos of Europe caused many parents to actually sell their daughters into slavery. The Jewish community preferred to ignore the fact that many young Jewish girls were becoming prostitutes. Bertha traveled throughout Europe exposing those who were involved in the profitable business of white slavery. She established a shelter called the Home for Wayward Girls and Illegitimate Babies to protect those who had been lured away from their families by false promises of jobs and marriage. She did not hesitate to denounce members of the Jewish community who supported the white-slave market because she believed "to know of wrong and to remain quiet is to share the guilt."

When she died of cancer in the spring of 1936, many

paid tribute to Bertha and praised her commitment to progress and the improvement of life for all people. Margarethe Susman, the poet, wrote:

> We all know that with the death of Bertha Pappenheim a great woman, a real fighter, a true Jewish person, has left us, that a life is gone which will not reappear in Judaism for generations, because of the drastically changed living conditions. We know her life was interwoven with a wide and fateful web of Jewish and German influences, that she lived through the developments of our times with an alert and passionate mind, never yielding her original position, no matter how intensely the changes of the era affected her. Her personality, her life, were from the beginning to the end a single flaming protest against the religious and moral dissolution of the time in which she lived. In the middle of all the uprooted, wavering, and tumbling lives in our world, she always stood erect and always progressed. For she possessed the highest gift that can be bestowed on a person, particularly those living in the chaos of enormous upheavals: a *way*. And this way was also a road for others. She led the way, pointing out the goals. She was gifted with great strength and the capacity to bring order to lives, to arrange them, to lead and train people. . . . This delicate woman took on the world.[6]

And Helene Hanna Thon, a Zionist leader, said:

> In these days of sorrow and suffering in Palestine, every person who feels bound to his brothers and sisters who need help is driven more than ever to the dwellings of the poorest in the country who—as everywhere in the world—are affected first by the misery of the times. When, then, I come home depressed from the sad experiences in the Jewish streets of the old town of Jerusalem and other districts of the poor to continue the work at my desk, there stands before me Bertha Pappenheim's picture, and as I study her features, the depression of the day falls away, and

there remains the recognition that beyond the harshness of our Jewish fate there is eternal immortal spirit.

The eyes of the woman in the picture below me have all their life looked deep into human suffering, human weakness, and immorality, until a reflection of all human sorrow resided in them. But they looked through this suffering, as through a transparent shell, until they reached the core of things: recognition of the immortal life of the Jewish people and of the immortal strength of Judaism.

When years ago I visited Bertha Pappenheim in the company of an eleven-year-old Palestinian boy, the child said, upon our leaving the room, "She looks like Deborah," so strongly had he been moved by the nobility of this face with its silvery white crown, resting on the delicate shoulders of the equally noble body.[7]

Bertha Pappenheim is not remembered only for her contributions to the field of social service. She also made a significant contribution to the development of psychoanalysis. It was her case history that led Freud to his discovery of the unconscious: she was Anna O. Remarkably, Freud never met her—he learned about her from Dr. Josef Breuer.

In 1880, Dr. Breuer was called to the Pappenheim home to treat Bertha for a nervous cough. He soon discovered, however, that she was suffering from what was then called hysteria. Through hypnosis, he stumbled on a method of treatment which Bertha later called her "talking cure." Soon afterward Breuer told Freud

how his patient's paralysis, poor vision, cough, muteness, and headaches had all disappeared under hypnosis as she talked about experiences related to each symptom. She was able to recall the first time the symptom had appeared and the emotions it provoked in her even though she had lost all conscious memory of the event and the emotions.[8]

Freud was fascinated, and the rest is history. Mental illness did not have an organic cause; its origin lay within the mind—and it was Bertha Pappenheim who led Freud to this monumental discovery.

Lucy Freeman concluded her biography of Bertha Pappenheim with these words:

> But she will never be forgotten by the world. She will be remembered as part of the history of Germany, of Vienna, of countries where families now live who are descended from a boy or girl she cared for at the Orphanage or Home, as well as those countries where volunteers trained by her and inspired by her devotion now work to help the oppressed and the needy.
>
> Most of all, she will be remembered by every man, woman, and child who has been, or ever will be, helped by psychoanalysis. In the achievement of Freud's monumental discoveries, ones that for the first time in history made possible the understanding of man's irrational behavior—war, murder, suicide, sexual perversions—Bertha Pappenheim was entitled to a share of the honor.
>
> "The very best a woman can do is to mean something to someone, and I am happy if I feel at times that I will not die, without having warmed someone at my small fire," she wrote. . . .
>
> Her "small fire" was to warm many as it helped ignite the blaze lit by Freud that illuminated heaven and hell —the unconscious mind of man.[9]

HANNAH SENESH

Hannah Senesh was born in Hungary and emigrated to Palestine in 1939. During World War II she served as a paratrooper in the British army. Having parachuted behind Nazi lines in Yugoslavia, she volunteered to cross the border to warn Hungarian Jews of the horrors to come. She was captured, however, and after unbearable torture at German hands was executed at the age of twenty-three.

Her diary provides us with a record of her strong sense of responsibility and of her courage.

Born on July 17, 1921, Hannah Senesh grew up in Budapest, where she lived with her mother and brother (her father died when she was six). She did not have a particularly Jewish upbringing. While her parents were definitely Jews, they did not see the importance of practicing ritual at home. Hannah, therefore, learned about Judaism at school. It was also at school that she first learned of anti-Semitism.

Hannah attended a private Protestant girls' school. When elections were being held for the literary society, she suddenly discovered that only Protestants could be elected. In her diary she wrote:

> Now I don't know how to behave toward the literary society. Should I put myself out and work for the improvement of the society's standards, even though I am now aware of the spirit that motivates it, or should I drop the whole thing? But if I drop it then I am going against the interests of my class. It is extremely difficult to find a way that is not demeaning, proud or isolationist, and also not forward. One has to be extremely careful before making any kind of move because one individual's faults can be generalized about. To my way of thinking, you have to be someone exceptional to fight anti-Semitism, which is the most difficult kind of fight. Only now am I beginning to see what it really means to be a Jew in a Christian society. But I don't mind at all. It is because we have to struggle, because it is more difficult for us to reach our goal, that we develop outstanding qualities.
>
> Had I been born a Christian, every profession would be open to me. I would become a teacher, and that would be the end of it. As it is, perhaps I'll succeed in getting into the profession for which, according to my abilities, I am best suited.
>
> Under no circumstances would I ever convert to Christianity, not only because of myself, but also because of

the children I hope one day to have. I would never force them into the ignoble position of having to deny or be ashamed of their origin. Nor would I rob them of their religion, which is what happens to the children of converted parents.

I think religion means a great deal in life, and I find the modern concept—that faith in God is only a crutch for the weak—ridiculous. It's exactly that faith which makes one strong, and because of it one does not depend upon other things for support.[10]

Later that year Hannah was elected an officer of the literary society, but was not permitted to serve. At last, she severed all connections with the organization.

By 1938 she had become a Zionist. She wrote in her diary:

I don't know whether I've already mentioned that I've become a Zionist. This word stands for a tremendous number of things. To me it means, in short, that I now consciously and strongly feel I am a Jew, and am proud of it. My primary aim is to go to Palestine, to work for it. Of course this did not develop from one day to the next; it was a somewhat gradual development. There was first talk of it about three years ago, and at that time I vehemently attacked the Zionist movement. Since then people, events, times have all brought me closer to the idea, and I am immeasurably happy that I've found this ideal, that I now feel firm ground under my feet, and can see a definite goal toward which it is really worth striving. I am going to start learning Hebrew, and I'll attend one of the youth groups. In short, I'm really going to knuckle down properly. I've become a different person, and it's a very good feeling.

One needs something to believe in, something for which one can have wholehearted enthusiasm. One needs to feel that one's life has meaning, that one is needed in this world. Zionism fulfills all this for me. One hears a good many arguments against the movement, but this doesn't matter. I believe in it, and that's the important thing.

I'm convinced Zionism is Jewry's solution to its problems, and that the outstanding work being done in Palestine is not in vain.[11]

By the time she was seventeen Hannah had decided to emigrate to Palestine. Her teachers made every attempt to prevent her from doing so. She had graduated at the top of her class and they were prepared to guarantee her acceptance at the university. But she rejected the life of a student, the life of an intellectual. She had dreams to fulfill. She wanted to help rebuild the homeland of her people. She left for Palestine on September 13, 1939, and ten days later in her diary, reflected on her decision:

Yesterday, on Yom Kippur Eve, I was very low. I mean spiritually. I made an accounting of what I had left behind, and what I had found here, and I didn't know whether the move would prove worthwhile. For a moment I lost sight of the goal. I deliberately let myself go because once in a while one must completely relax from all one's tensions and from being constantly on guard. It felt good to let go, to cry for once. But even behind the tears I felt I had done the right thing. This is where my life's ambition—I might even say my vocation—binds me; because I would like to feel that by being here I am fulfilling a mission, not just vegetating. Here almost every life is the fulfillment of a mission.[12]

The diary continues with a vivid description of life in Palestine, of training at an agricultural school, of traveling, and of days in the *kibbutz*. By 1942 she was anxious to enlist in the *Palmach*, the Jewish self-defense force in Palestine. She also thought of returning to Hungary to help organize youth emigration and to rescue her mother. When a group was organized for this purpose in 1943, she recorded her willingness to serve:

I see the hand of destiny in this just as I did at the time of my *aliyah* [immigration]. I wasn't master of my fate then either. I was enthralled by one idea, and it gave me no rest. I knew I would emigrate, despite the many obstacles in my path. Now I again sense the excitement of something important and vital ahead, and the feeling of inevitability connected with a decisive and urgent step. The entire plan may miscarry, and I may receive a brief notification informing me that the matter will be postponed, or that I don't qualify. But I think I have the capabilities necessary for just this assignment, and I'll fight for it with all my might.[13]

Despite her fears Hannah was accepted, and soon afterward began her training as a paratrooper in the British army. Her optimism was a source of strength for her comrades; her courage was amazing. The small group of parachutists were sent to Yugoslavia, but she was anxious to cross the border into Hungary. She told her comrades:

We are the only ones who can possibly help, we don't have the right to think of our own safety; we don't have the right to hesitate. Even if the chances of our success are minuscule, we must go. If we don't go for fear of our lives, a million Jews will surely be massacred. If we succeed, our work can open great and important avenues of activity. Thanks to our efforts, multitudes will be saved. It's better to die and free our conscience than to return with the knowledge that we didn't even try.[14]

After crossing the border into Hungary, Hannah was captured and imprisoned by the Germans. She remained in good spirits, however, and spent her time encouraging others. One of her comrades wrote about her:

She found an ingenious way of communicating with prisoners whose cell windows faced hers by cutting out large letters and placing them, one after the other, in her window to form words. In this way she introduced herself to the prisoners, learned their troubles, gave them information about happenings outside the prison walls, and also told them about Palestine and *kibbutz* life. Her window became an information and education center, and from morning till evening prisoners looked toward it for news. Opposite her were some members of the Zionist movement who had been arrested for underground activities and were awaiting sentence. She encouraged them, gave them new heart.

Her behavior before members of the Gestapo and SS was quite remarkable. She always stood up to them, warning them plainly of the bitter fate they would suffer after their defeat. Curiously, these wild animals, in whom every spark of humanity had been extinguished, felt awed in the presence of this refined, fearless young girl. They knew she was Jewish, but they knew also that she was a British paratrooper who had come to fight them. Having been taught for years that Jews never fight back, that they will accept the vilest treatment, they were taken aback by her courage. The warden of the prison, a notorious sadist who was credited with the death of many he had tortured with his own hands, considered it a privilege to visit her cell daily to argue with her fearless criticism of German rule and her prophecies of an Allied victory.[15]

Nonetheless, Hannah suffered brutal tortures. They tied her, whipped her, and beat her. They forced her to sit completely still for hours on end. They demanded her radio code, but she refused to tell it to them. Even when they took her to Budapest and told her that they had imprisoned her mother, she remained silent. One of her comrades described the incident.

The Germans knew their business. They threatened that if she did not reveal her secret, they would torture her mother before her eyes and kill her. Still Hannah would not yield. Only someone who knows how deeply she loved her mother can fathom what went on in her heart. I was completely shattered on hearing her story and stared at her in astonishment. How could she have remained so resolute and calm? Where did this girl, who loved her mother so much, find the courage to sacrifice her, too, if necessary, rather than reveal the secret that was not hers, that affected the lives of so many? As it was, Hannah's fortitude saved her mother. Had she broken down and surrendered her secret, they would doubtless have executed her immediately and sent her mother off to the chambers of Auschwitz.

But the Germans didn't give up. They kept Hannah and her mother in the same prison, believing that prison, hunger, and fear of death would humble her.[16]

Hannah Senesh never gave in. When she was brought to trial, she refused to ask for clemency and was executed. Her final words to her comrades were: "Continue on the way, don't be deterred. Continue the struggle till the end, until the day of liberty comes, the day of victory for our people."

She was buried, although no one knows by whom, in the martyrs' section of the Jewish Cemetery in Budapest. Later her body was moved to Israel, where it was buried in the national military cemetery with the highest military honors. Leading members of the government attended the ceremony and paid tribute to her memory. She is considered a national heroine, and most Israelis are familiar with her diary and poems. In fact, nearly every Israeli, young or old, can recite from memory her poem "Blessed is the Match":

Blessed is the match consumed in kindling flame.
Blessed is the flame that burns in the secret fastness of the heart.
Blessed is the heart with strength to stop its beating for honor's sake.
Blessed is the match consumed in kindling flame.[17]

The words of another of her poems have become a popular prayer among American Jews:

Eli, Eli, shelo y'gamer l'olam,
Hachol v'hayam,
Rish-rush shel hamayim,
B'rak hashamayim,
Tefillat haadam.

O Lord, my God, I pray that these things never end:
The sand and the sea,
The rush of the waters,
The crash of the heavens,
The human prayer.[18]

Hannah Senesh possessed unlimited courage. She earned her place among the martyrs of our people. Perhaps the greatest tribute that can be paid to her are words she herself wrote at the beginning of her diary:

There are stars whose radiance is visible on earth though they have long been extinct. There are people whose brilliance continues to light the world though they are no longer among the living. These lights are particularly bright when the night is dark. They light the way for humanity.[19]

GOLDA MEIR

In 1906, Blume Mabovitz joined her husband Moshe in America. They had fled the Russian pogroms and would now settle in Milwaukee with their three daughters, one of whom was named Golda. Golda realized almost immediately that America gave citizens the opportunity to speak out against social injustice. At the age of ten she turned her attention to those among her classmates who could not afford schoolbooks. She taught English to immigrants at 10 cents a lesson, using the money to organize her friends into the American Young Sister Society whose goal it was to buy books for the needy. At twelve she spoke on a street corner in support of the Socialist Party, and by the time she graduated from school she had already formed her own philosophy:

> Only those who dare, who have the courage to dream, can really accomplish something. People who are forever asking themselves: "Is it realistic? Can it be accomplished? Is it worth trying?" accomplish nothing that's really worthwhile or imaginative. What's realistic? A stone? Something that's already in existence? That's not realism. That's death. It's stagnation.[20]

At the age of seventeen Golda was raising funds to help the Jews of Eastern Europe. But now she encountered anti-Semitism in the United States. Many Americans, she found, were lobbying for the exclusion of Jewish immigrants. As a result, Golda turned to Zionism. She began to realize the importance of an independent land where Jews might live in freedom. She argued the need for Jews themselves to rebuild the land. Following the passage of the Balfour Declaration, she convinced her rather reluctant fiancé, Moshe Myerson, to make *aliyah*. (In fact, she had insisted that his promise to emigrate with her be included in their marriage vows.) She firmly believed that an advocate of Zionism had to live in the Jewish homeland.

When they arrived in Palestine the Myersons sought to join Kibbutz Merhavia, but the members were less than cordial. They assumed that Golda, a "pampered American girl," would never be able to endure the difficult *kibbutz* life. They couldn't have been more wrong. Even in those early days Golda exhibited the stamina that would later allow Israel's first woman prime minister to attend every cabinet meeting, make several speeches a week throughout the country, and visit the troops in the field.

She took her turn cleaning the barn, feeding the animals, and clearing the land to plant saplings. When she was assigned to the kitchen to do what others called "women's work," she used her imagination to improve the quality and appearance of the food. And while everyone else wore unironed clothing, Golda wore a neatly ironed dress (the ironing was done in her own room on her own time).

Golda felt great joy in knowing that everything she did was contributing to the rebuilding of the land, but Moshe, her husband, was very unhappy with *kibbutz* life and so they moved to Tel Aviv and later to Jerusalem, where Golda attempted to be simply a housewife. But she was the type of woman whose nature demanded more than children and a family life. It was not long before she became involved in the affairs of the growing country. Her first appointment was as secretary of the women's Labor Council of *Histadrut,* the national labor federation. Terry Morris explains her role:

> [The Women's Labor Council] members were young women from Jewish middle-class families in Europe who had come to Palestine to help create a new social order with guarantees of full emancipation and equality for women. Few of them had any training in agriculture or, for that matter, in any of the skills needed for the evolution of the new society. Golda's task was to help establish training farms for the girls and such backup communal facilities as nurseries and kindergartens for the children of working women.[21]

In many ways, Golda Meir was a forerunner of today's feminist movement, although she always took feminine equality for granted. She once said:

> All my adult life I have worked among men, and they have treated me on my merits. I never knew a man who gave in to an argument of mine because I was a woman

—except one, my husband—and they had the open-mindedness and the manliness to accept my idea if they thought it was right. I always tried to reciprocate—I didn't expect privileges because I was a woman, and if the majority was against me, I accepted it, even if I knew it was a man's idea . . . and wrong.

I think women often get not so much an unfair deal as an illogical one. Once in the cabinet we had to deal with the fact that there had been an outbreak of assaults on women at night. One minister (a member of an extreme religious party) suggested a curfew. Women should stay home after dark. I said: "But it's the men who are attacking the women. If there's to be a curfew, let the men stay at home, not the women." [22]

Her decision to become active in public life caused Golda to neglect her family somewhat, but she has always believed that a woman given the opportunity to develop her potential brings more to her children than the woman forced to remain at home. Her daughter evidently agrees with her. When asked if she resented her mother's lack of attention, she replied: "For such a mother it was worth it."

Golda Meir served her chosen country in many ways. In 1947 she was called upon to head the Jewish Agency's political department. As a result it was her job to convince the Cyprus refugees awaiting entrance to Israel that those families with children should be given priority on the immigration quota. She later described this experience:

These people came from camps in Germany behind barbed wire to camps in Cyprus behind barbed wire. There was not a blade of grass, just miserable tents, yet some of our people had gone to live there and help out. I wonder how they could live there. There were children in Cyprus who had never seen a live flower. They had never held a rose or any other flower in their hands. But our volunteer kindergarten teachers taught them how to make flowers out of paper, and when I arrived on the island, a child gave me a whole bouquet of paper flowers. No bouquet I have ever received or ever shall receive will be more beautiful than the paper flowers from the children of Cyprus.[23]

It became another of Golda's prime responsibilities to raise funds from American Jews. In January 1948 she arrived in the United States to appeal for money to be used for arms. She was told not to expect more than $5 to $7 million but that did not discourage her. She went to a conference of the Council of Jewish Federations in Chicago and in her own inimitable way she stood before the audience and said:

> I came for this very simple thing: to get in cash, in two or three weeks, $25 million. Very simple. Since I have no idea what $25 million really means, what it looks like, I know from nothing: I need $25 million in a few weeks.[24]

Honest and forthright, she spoke from the heart:

> Every Jew in the country knows that within a few months a Jewish state in Palestine will be established. We have to pay for it. We know that the price we have to pay will be the lives of the best of our people. But there is no doubt that the spirit of our young people will not falter. The spirit is there. But this spirit alone cannot face rifles and machine guns. Rifles and machine guns without spirit are not worth very much, but spirit without these in time can be broken with the body. . . . You cannot decide whether we will fight or not. We will. No white flag of the Jewish community will be raised. The decision is taken. Nobody can change that. You can change only one thing—whether we shall be victorious. Yes, whether we fight or not, this is a decision we have to make. Whether we live or not, this is a decision you have to make.[25]

As simple as her speech had been, the response was equally simple: the $25 million was made available immediately.

After Israel's independence was proclaimed, Golda was appointed ambassador to Moscow. She didn't want to accept the position because it meant that she would have to leave Israel, but she knew that it was important to acknowledge Soviet recognition of the Jewish state. And so she went.

On Yom Kipper in Moscow she decided to attend a religious service. It was normal then for about two thousand people to attend services, but when word got out that Golda was coming, over forty thousand Russian Jews gathered at the synagogue. Terry Morris explains what happened when the congregation got to the prayer *L'shana ha-ba'ah b'Yerushalayim* ("Next year in Jerusalem"):

> The voices shook the synagogue and all eyes were raised to Golda.
> Golda said, through tears, "This is the most passionate Zionist speech I have ever heard."
> Apparently, the Soviet Government had failed in more than thirty years of effort to wipe out Zionist sympathies among Russian Jewry.
> "The privilege and heartbreaking experience I had with Soviet Jewry," Golda said later, "made me more certain of the survival of Soviet Jewry than I am of Jewry in some free countries. Not because that Jewry is better, but because I think that throughout our history it has been proven that outside forces, no matter how brutal, cannot force the Jews to stop being Jews. The only ones who can decide on assimilation, and assimilate, are Jews themselves, of their own free will." [26]

Mrs. Meir later served Israel as foreign minister. Under her leadership the hand of friendship was offered to other nations—particularly those in Africa. Under an international cooperation program, Israeli experts shared their knowledge in the fields of agriculture, medicine and health, education, and technology. At one point Billy Graham asked Golda: "How do you account for the success of your program especially in Africa?" And she answered, as she alone could, "That's easy. We go there to teach, not to preach."

In 1961 Golda welcomed Afro-Asian delegations to Haifa for a seminar on the role of women in a developing society. One group of representatives sent her this letter:

> We are now more aware of problems existing in our own countries. We have more courage to face the challenges and to realize that we women, as educators of the nation, should no longer expect to be spoonfed or wait for manna to fall from heaven. Having been to Israel, to this land of promise, flowing with milk and honey, we are quite full of inspiration to return home and get down to the task of working out our future heritage.[27]

Golda Meir retired in 1966 and again in 1968. But when Prime Minister Levi Eshkol died, the leaders of the labor party Mapai were certain that Golda was the only one who could form an acceptable coalition government. Not everyone agreed. Still, on March 17, 1969, she presented her nominations for the cabinet to the *Knesset* and received the largest vote of confidence of any government since Israel's independence. Some thought of her as an old, sick woman. Many thought she would be only an interim prime minister. But her amazing ability to lead, her stamina, and her sincerity enabled her to govern for five years.

Before, in 1959, she had accepted the Stephen Wise Award of the American Jewish Congress, saying:

> It has been my happy fortune to go all the way from that small room in a despotic land (Russia) to life in the State of Israel, where there are a great workers' movement, humane workers' enterprises, agricultural settlements, and the cooperatives of the *kibbutz* and *moshav*. If a Jewish woman who was a child in that

little room lives to be blessed with a daughter and grandchildren living in a *kibbutz* under a system that cannot be surpassed for equality and respect for human dignity, what more can she desire? . . .

Perhaps you will think it just pretense—but believe me, on no day of my life have I said to myself in a mood of self-satisfaction, "Well, today I've done something for the people of Israel, the State of Israel." I have always been aware that I have been boundlessly blessed by the experiences granted me. . . .

For myself, after all that I have known, I desire only one thing more: to live only as long as I can live a full life in the State of Israel and never lose the feeling that it is I who am indebted for what has been given me.[28]

POINT OF VIEW

Apologists would say that these examples provide ample proof that women who desired to do so could make it in a man's world. But these women are exceptions to the rule; they give evidence of tokenism rather than acceptance. We don't desire what we think is impossible, and until recent times it is highly unlikely that many Jewish women dreamed of an equal place in a male-dominated society.

That most of us have never heard of Ernestine Rose, Bertha Pappenheim, or Hannah Senesh is evidence of our failure to provide a variety of role models for our daughters. Too many textbooks put women "in their place" and never allow them to seek fulfillment outside the home. But women also possess basic human qualities such as the desire for power, ambition, strength, and independence; and unless we teach about heroines as well as heroes, we stifle our daughters' curiosity and suppress their imagination.

They can become aware of life's possibilities by knowing that women *have* made significant contributions in every field of human endeavor. If we make a conscious effort to provide a variety of role models, then they will know that they do not have to conceal other desires and dreams for the sake of marriage and a family and they will be encouraged to express themselves in ways that truly suit their personalities.

4

CREATING
TOMORROW'S
JEWISH
WOMAN

CHAPTER NINE
More than Token Equality

We have now examined the role of women in Jewish tradition. While women have always been honored and respected, they have definitely held a secondary position to that of men. In many cases, their rights as human beings have been ignored. At the same time, the Jewish community has often been far ahead of other cultures in its treatment of women. This does not excuse the inequality that has existed, but it does challenge us once again to take the lead in coming to terms with the developments of the past century. Token equality is not enough. Changes will have to be made if at last we are to take our rightful places among the people of Israel.

MARRIAGE AND DIVORCE

Jewish laws concerning marriage and divorce are an insult to the dignity of woman. To continue to regard women as possessions is not only humiliating but contrary to the spirit of our tradition. Jewish law has never been static. The rabbis of the Talmud made changes in biblical law when the situation demanded them. Later sages and scholars discussed the decisions of the rabbis and again modified the law when necessary. Therefore, there is no reason why *Halachah* cannot be reinterpreted to grant women legal equality with regard to divorce and *halitsah* and to free the many women who suffer under the laws of the *agunah*. Ethical statements advising husbands to honor and respect their wives are no substitute for the right to divorce and remarry when one chooses to do so. The time has come to change those laws that so obviously protect the rights of men and to allow women to control their own destinies.

EDUCATION

Religious school education seeks to encourage Jewish identification and participation on the part of our young people. Existing curricula, however, often fail to support this goal when it comes to Jewish girls. Traditional stereotypes are constantly enforced and our daughters are made to feel from the first day of their education that their place is in the home. Textbooks abound with examples of women fulfilling their household responsibilities so that dinner will be ready when their husbands come home from synagogue. Little boys learn how to build a *sukkah* while little girls are taught to bake *hallah*. In course after course our children learn about the heroes of our people but almost nothing about the heroines. As a result, our daughters have no role models to identify with; they are not inspired and urged to develop their creative potential to its fullest. The only way we can remedy this situation is to rewrite our textbooks and to provide courses of study for young people and adults that take into account the tremendous number of contributions made by Jewish women to the Jewish community and to the history of humanity. Unless this is done, the traditional stereotypes will be reinforced and we shall run the risk of turning away our young people who are struggling to establish their identities in an ever-changing world.

CUSTOMS AND CEREMONIES

Once again, Jewish girls find little encouragement when they seek to participate in customs and ceremonies. Authority figures within the synagogue are male, and girls are often not given the opportunity to use skills they have been taught in our religious schools. In many instances they are not given *aliyot;* they are not permitted to read from the Torah; they are not allowed to conduct the service. Even in some Reform congregations, *Bat Mitzvah* ceremonies are not available for girls or if they are, they are not comparable to the ceremony in which boys participate. In more traditional congregations, where the *Bar Mitzvah* marks the entrance of the boy into the life of the synagogue, all too often the *Bat Mitzvah* marks the end of a girl's participation. She knows that she may never again be asked to ascend the pulpit except perhaps to bless the candles on Sisterhood Sabbath.

If true equality is to be gained, then our daughters must be made to feel that their spiritual development is as important as that of their brothers. The birth of a daughter should be as significant as the birth of a son; the joyous celebration that now takes place at the time of a boy's circumcision should occur instead at the naming of the child, either girl or boy. The entrance of our daughters and our sons into the covenant of our tradition should be marked with an equal ceremony.

Girls must have the same opportunity as boys to obtain recognition for the studies they have completed through participating in a *Bat Mitzvah* ceremony equal to a *Bar Mitzvah*. Wedding ceremonies should stress the importance of respecting the uniqueness of each partner.

Women should be permitted to participate in every aspect of synagogue ritual. They should be counted in the *minyan,* encouraged to read from the Torah, and permitted to carry the Scrolls during the *hakafot* (procession) on *Simhat Torah.* The obligation to recite *Kaddish* should also be theirs, and the liturgy should be rewritten to eliminate male-oriented language. Thus, "mankind" and "fathers" should give way to "humanity" and "ancestors."

The society in which we live no longer demands that women be exempt from all positive time-bound commandments. Rather, our way of life demands full and equal responsibility.

POSITIONS OF LEADERSHIP

Women should be permitted to occupy positions of leadership in every aspect of the Jewish community. All too often women are appointed to serve on synagogue boards of trustees as representatives of the sisterhood or the religious school. Seldom are they elected in their own right, and they rarely serve on nominating committees. The same is true of community organizations. For too many years women have been relegated to the role of "cookie ladies." If equality is to be more than just a word, we must actively seek qualified women who will bring their knowledge and expertise to the highest levels of leadership in all our organizations. The opportunity to serve can no longer be tied to the ability to contribute financially. Women have too much to offer to be confined solely to women's divisions. Jacqueline K. Levine expressed the need for increased participation and opportunity this way:

> Seven years ago last March I participated in the glorious march from Selma to Montgomery, a march undertaken for the purpose of securing voting rights for all

Americans. I stood, one balmy Alabama night, under a starry Alabama sky, and I heard the never-to-be-for-gotten voice of Martin Luther King ring out in his never-to-be-heard-again prophetic cadences as he said, "We are all witnesses together." He did not mean witness as onlooker, witness as voyeur. He meant wit-ness—participant. And so are we women, when we ask to share in communal responsibility, asking to be witnesses, participants, in our own Jewish community. We are asking that there be developed a real com-munity. We are asking that our talents of maintaining Jewish life through the centuries—of caring for our children, of developing a volunteer cadre capable of remarkable achievement, of welding realism with com-passion, of developing a real understanding of the priorities a society should have—not be set aside any longer on the grounds of a prefabricated sexual role difference. We are asking, in short, to be treated only as human beings, so that we may be witness to and par-ticipants in the exciting challenge of creating a new and open and total Jewish community.[1]

CONSCIOUSNESS-RAISING

How are we to accomplish the above goals? Women must take the initiative. No matter how loud the cry for female equality, nothing will be accomplished if there are no women who want to serve on congregational boards or become rabbis or share in the decision-making process of religious institutions. Resolutions in favor of increased participation on the part of women will mean little if women are reluctant to accept new roles. Continued con-sciousness-raising is an important tool in facing this obsta-cle. Women must constantly be made aware of their potential as an influential force in the survival of our people; they must be convinced that they are capable of accepting positions of leadership.

Change comes about only when those who are being

discriminated against demand it. The following incident was described in the Book of Numbers. A man named Zelophechad died, leaving no sons, but five daughters. According to biblical law, only sons could inherit their father's property. The daughters of Zelophechad disagreed with this law and they sought to change it. They appeared before Moses and they asked: "Why should the name of our father be done away from among his family because he had no son? Let us inherit his land." Moses pondered the matter and consulted God and God said: "The daughters of Zelophechad are right. Give them possession of their father's land." And so the law was changed. Women who saw themselves as an oppressed minority went to Moses and insisted that he do something about it. Similarly, the complete equality that justice demands will never really be achieved until women sit down with individual rabbis and boards of trustees and demand the right to be involved in every aspect of the synagogue and the Jewish community. Only then will we have religious institutions and organizations that are truly sensitive to the needs of all their congregants and members, and that reflect the creative talents and skills of all who wish to participate.

Notes

CHAPTER ONE: THE BIBLICAL CONCEPT OF WOMANHOOD

1. Hayyim Schauss, *The Lifetime of a Jew* (New York: Union of American Hebrew Congregations, 1950), pp. 71–72.
2. Mary Gendler, " 'Male and Female Created He Them': A Feminist View," *Jewish Heritage,* Winter 1971/72, pp. 24–29.
3. Mary Gendler, "The Vindication of Vashti," *Response,* Summer 1973, pp. 154–60.
4. Louis M. Epstein, *Marriage Laws in the Bible and the Talmud* (Cambridge: Harvard University Press, 1942), p. 7.
5. Trude Weiss-Rosmarin, "The Seventh Commandment," *Jewish Spectator,* October 1971, pp. 1–5.
6. Epstein, *Marriage Laws,* pp. 127–28.
7. *Rabbi's Manual* (New York: Central Conference of American Rabbis, 1961), p. 135.

CHAPTER TWO: RABBINIC ATTITUDES TOWARD WOMEN

1. Louis M. Epstein, *The Jewish Marriage Contract* (New York: Jewish Theological Seminary of America, 1927), p. 2.
2. Ibid., p. 147.

CHAPTER THREE: EMANCIPATION BRINGS CHANGES

1. "Report of Committee on Ordination of Women," *CCAR Yearbook,* vol. 66 (Philadelphia: Central Conference of American Rabbis, 1956), p. 91.

2. W. Gunther Plaut, *The Rise of Reform Judaism* (New York: Union of American Hebrew Congregations, 1963), pp. 253–55.

3. "Report of Committee on Ordination of Women," p. 90.

4. W. Gunther Plaut, *The Growth of Reform Judaism* (New York: Union of American Hebrew Congregations, 1965), pp. 339–40.

5. Mordecai M. Kaplan, *The Future of the American Jew* (New York: Reconstructionist Press, 1948), p. 402.

CHAPTER FOUR: CREATION OF THE STATE OF ISRAEL

1. Molly Lyons Bar-David, *Women in Israel* (New York: Hadassah, 1952), p. 8.

2. Ada Maimon, *Women Build a Land,* trans. Shulamith Schwarz-Nardi (New York: Herzl Press, 1962), p. 26.

3. Ibid., p. 37.

4. Bar-David, *Women in Israel,* pp. 21–22.

5. Maimon, *Women Build a Land,* p. 74.

6. Ibid., p. 152.

7. Ibid., p. 83.

8. Ibid., p. 208.

9. Ibid., p. 246.

10. Ibid., pp. 244–45.

11. Bar-David, *Women in Israel,* p. 75.

12. Shulamit Aloni, "Israeli Women Need Liberation," *Sisters of Exile: Sources on the Jewish Woman* (New York: Ichud Habonim Labor Zionist Youth, 1973), p. 143.

13. Ibid., p. 146.

CHAPTER FIVE: RITUAL

1. Marvin Lowenthal, *Henrietta Szold, Life and Letters* (New York: The Viking Press, 1942), pp. 92–93.

2. "Report of Committee on Ordination of Women," *CCAR Yearbook,* vol. 66 (Philadelphia: Central Conference of American Rabbis, 1956), pp. 90–91.

3. Martha Neumark, "The Woman Rabbi," *The Jewish Tribune,* 10 April 1925.

4. Idem.

5. Jacob Z. Lauterbach, "Responsum on Question, 'Shall

Women Be Ordained Rabbis?'" *CCAR Yearbook,* vol. 32 (1922), pp. 161–62.
6. David Neumark, *CCAR Yearbook,* vol. 32, p. 177.
7. Jacob R. Marcus, "The First Woman Rabbi," *The American Israelite,* 9 March 1972.

CHAPTER SIX: ECONOMIC AND CULTURAL CONTRIBUTIONS

1. Mark Zborowski and Elizabeth Herzog, *Life Is with People* (New York: Schocken Books, 1962), pp. 130–31.
2. Ibid., pp. 140–41.
3. *The First Fifty Years* (New York: National Council of Jewish Women, 1943), p. 35.
4. Ibid., pp. 70–71.
5. *Women's World,* June 1974, p. 7.
6. Jacqueline K. Levine, "The Changing Role of Women in the Jewish Community," *Response,* Summer 1973, pp. 62–63.

CHAPTER SEVEN: THE JEWISH MOTHER STEREOTYPE

1. Herman Wouk, *Marjorie Morningstar* (New York: Doubleday & Company, 1955), pp. 171–72.
2. Ibid., pp. 172–73.
3. Leslie A. Fiedler, *Love and Death in the American Novel* (New York: Stein & Day, 1966), p. 255.
4. Marie Syrkin, "The Fun of Self-Abuse," *Midstream,* April 1969, pp. 64–65.
5. Bruno Bettelheim, "Portnoy Psychoanalyzed," *Midstream,* June/July 1969, p. 9.
6. Arthur J. Lelyveld, "Old Disease in New Form: Diagnosing *Portnoy's Complaint,*" *The Jewish Digest,* June 1969, p. 2.
7. Zena Smith Blau, "In Defense of the Jewish Mother," *Midstream,* February 1967, p. 47.
8. Ibid., pp. 46–47.
9. Ibid., p. 45.
10. Ibid., p. 44.
11. Ibid., p. 47.

CHAPTER EIGHT: GREAT JEWISH WOMEN

1. Yuri Suhl, *Eloquent Crusader, Ernestine Rose* (New York: Julian Messner, 1970), p. 105.

2. Ibid., p. 106.

3. Ibil., pp. 154–55.

4. Ibid., p. 172.

5. Lucy Freeman, *The Story of Anna O.* (New York: Walker and Company, 1972), pp. 64–65.

6. Ibid., p. 176.

7. Ibid., p. 179.

8. Ibid., p. 187.

9. Ibid., p. 266.

10. *Hannah Senesh, Her Life and Diary,* trans. Marta Cohn (New York: Schocken Books, 1971), p. 32.

11. Ibid., p. 63.

12. Ibid., p. 81.

13. Ibid., p. 127.

14. Ibid., p. 186.

15. Ibid., p. 190.

16. Ibid., p. 194.

17. Ibid., p. 256.

18. Ibid., p. 254.

19. Ibid., p. 13.

20. Terry Morris, *Shalom, Golda* (New York: Hawthorn Books, 1971), p. 14.

21. Ibid., p. 63.

22. Golda Meir, *A Land of Our Own,* ed. Marie Syrkin (New York: G. P. Putnam's Sons, 1973), p. 240.

23. Morris, *Shalom, Golda,* p. 92.

24. Ibid., p. 98.

25. Ibid., pp. 98–99.

26. Ibid., p. 121.

27. Ibid., p. 152.

28. Meir, *A Land of Our Own,* pp. 237–39.

CHAPTER NINE: MORE THAN TOKEN EQUALITY

1. Jacqueline K. Levine, "The Changing Role of Women in the Jewish Community," *Response,* Summer 1973, pp. 64–65.

The Introduction is adapted from my article, "Not for Men Only," in *Council Woman,* February 1974, pp. 10–12.

Remarks in Chapter Three are adapted from my article, "From Promise to Reality," in *Keeping Posted,* April 1972, pp. 17–19.

Suggested Readings

GENERAL ANTHOLOGIES

The Jewish Woman, An Anthology. Response, Summer 1973.

Jung, Rabbi Leo. *The Jewish Library.* Vol. 3. New York: Soncino, 1970.

Sisters of Exile: Sources on the Jewish Woman. New York: Ichud Habonim Labor Zionist Youth, 1973.

WOMEN IN JEWISH RELIGION, LAW, AND TEXTS

Adler, Rachel. "The Jew Who Wasn't There: Halacha and the Jewish Woman." *Davka,* Summer 1971, pp. 6–11.

Brin, Ruth F. "Can a Woman Be a Jew?" *Reconstructionist,* 25 October 1968, pp. 7–14.

Davidowicz, Lucy S. "On Being a Woman in Shul." *Commentary,* July 1968, pp. 71–74.

Epstein, Louis M. *The Jewish Marriage Contract.* New York: Jewish Theological Seminary of America, 1927.

———. *Marriage Laws in the Bible and the Talmud.* Cambridge: Harvard University Press, 1942.

Ezekiel, Ezekiel Moses. "The Position of Woman in Rabbinical Literature." 3 pts. *Journal of the Bombay Branch of the Royal Asiatic Society,* 1927.

Feldman, David M. *Birth Control in Jewish Law.* New York: New York University Press, 1968.

Gendler, Mary. "Male and Female Created He Them." *Jewish Heritage,* Winter 1971/72, pp. 24–29.

————. Symposium Essay. *Response,* Winter 1970/71. pp. 35–40.

Gittelsohn, Roland B. "Women's Lib and Judaism." *Midstream,* October 1971, pp. 51–58.

Goldman, Rachel. "The Liberation of the Yiddisha Mama." *The Village Voice,* 11 February 1971.

Greenberg, Simon. "And He Writes Her a Bill of Divorcement." *Conservative Judaism,* Spring 1970, pp. 75–141.

Hauptman, Judith. "Women's Liberation in the Talmudic Period: An Assessment." *Conservative Judaism,* Summer 1972, pp. 22–28.

Hirschowitz, Rabbi Abraham E. *Yohale Sarah Containing Religious Duties of the Daughters of Israel and Moral Helps.* New York, 1918.

Hoenig, Rabbi Sidney B. *Jewish Family Life: The Duty of the Woman.* New York: The Spero Foundation, 1963.

Hyman, Paula. "The Other Half: Women in the Jewish Tradition." *Conservative Judaism,* Summer 1972, pp. 14–21.

Loewe, Raphael. *The Position of Women in Judaism.* London: Hazell Watson & Viney, 1966.

MacDonald, Elizabeth Mary. *The Position of Women as Reflected in Semitic Codes of Law.* Toronto: The University of Toronto Press, 1931.

Maimonides. *The Book of Women.* New Haven: Yale University Press, 1972.

"Report of Committee on Ordination of Women." *CCAR Yearbook,* Vol. 66. Philadelphia: Central Conference of American Rabbis, 1956, pp. 90–93.

"Responsum on Question 'Shall Women be Ordained Rabbis?'" Jacob Z. Lauterbach. *CCAR Yearbook,* Vol. 32. Richmond: Central Conference of American Rabbis, 1922, pp. 156–77.

Solis-Cohen, Jr., Emily. *Woman in Jewish Law and Life.* New York: Jewish Publication Society of America, 1932.

Weiss-Rosmarin, Trude. "The Seventh Commandment." *Jewish Spectator,* October 1971, pp. 1–5.

————. "The Unfreedom of Jewish Women." *Jewish Spectator,* October 1970, pp. 31f.

————. "Women in the Jewish Community." *Jewish Spectator,* February 1972, pp. 6–8.

Weissman, Deborah. "Toward a Feminist Critique of Judaism." *Congress Bi-Weekly,* 24 November 1972.

Zborowski, Mark and Herzog, Elizabeth. *Life Is with People.* New York: Schocken Books, 1962.

Zucrow, Solomon. *Women, Slaves, and the Ignorant in Rabbinic Literature.* Boston: The Stratford Company, 1932.

BIOGRAPHICAL SKETCHES

Arendt, Hannah. *Rahel Varnhagen, The Life of a Jewish Woman.* New York: Harcourt Brace Jovanovich, 1974.

Blau, Zena Smith. "In Defense of the Jewish Mother." *Midstream,* February 1967, pp. 42–50.

Drinnon, Richard. *Rebel in Paradise: A Biography of Emma Goldman.* Chicago: University of Chicago Press, 1961.

Fineman, Irving. *Woman of Valor—Life of Henrietta Szold.* New York: Simon & Schuster, 1961.

Freeman, Lucy. *The Story of Anna O.* New York: Walker and Company, 1972.

Gluckel of Hameln. *Life of Gluckel of Hameln, Written by Herself.* London: East and West Library, 1962.

Goldman, Emma. *Living My Life.* 2 vols. New York: Dover Publications, 1971.

Jacob, H. E. *The World of Emma Lazarus.* New York: Schocken Books, 1949.

Kobler, Franz., ed. *Her Children Call Her Blessed.* New York: Stephen Daye Press, 1955.

Lebeson, Anita Libman. *Recall to Life—The Jewish Woman in America.* New York: Thomas Yoseloff, 1970.

Lowenthal, Marvin. *Henrietta Szold, Life and Letters.* New York: The Viking Press, 1942.

Meir, Golda. *A Land of Our Own.* Edited by Marie Syrkin. New York: G. P. Putnam's Sons, 1973.

Morris, Terry. *Shalom, Golda.* New York: Hawthorn Books, 1971.

Raddock, Charles. "Once There Was a Female Chassidic Rabbi." *The Jewish Digest,* December 1967, pp. 20–24.

Senesh, Hannah. *Hannah Senesh, Her Life and Diary.* Translated by Marta Cohn. New York: Schocken Books 1972.

Stadtler, Bea. *The Adventures of Gluckel of Hameln.* New York: United Synagogue Commission on Jewish Education, 1967.

————. *The Story of Dona Gracia Mendes.* New York: United Synagogue Commission on Jewish Education, 1969.

Suhl, Yuri. *Eloquent Crusader, Ernestine Rose.* New York: Julian Messner, 1970.

Syrkin, Marie. *Blessed Is the Match.* Philadelphia: Jewish Publication Society, 1947.

Wald, Lillian. *The House on Henry Street.* New York: Holt, 1915.

ORGANIZATIONS

Comay, Joan. *The Hadassah Story.* Jerusalem: Information Services, Hadassah Council in Israel, 1958.

The First Fifty Years. New York: National Council of Jewish Women, 1944.

Grusd, Edward E. *B'nai B'rith: The Story of a Covenant.* New York: Appleton-Century, 1966.

Horowitz, Gloria Goldreich. *The Hadassah Idea: History and Development.* New York: Hadassah, 1966.

Jacobson, Ruth. *Manual for Sisterhoods.* New York: National Federation of Temple Sisterhoods, 1954.

Rader, Jack. *By the Skill of Their Hands: The Story of ORT.* Geneva: World ORT Union, 1970.

ISRAEL

Aloni, Shulamit. "Israel's Women Need Women's Lib." *Israel* magazine, April 1971, pp. 58–68.

————. "The Status of the Woman in Israel." *Judaism,* Spring 1973, pp. 248–56.

Bar-David, Molly Lyons. *Women in Israel.* New York: Hadassah, 1952.

Elizur, Judith Neulander. "Women in Israel." *Judaism,* Spring 1973, pp. 237–47.

Katznelson-Rubashow, Rachel. *The Ploughwoman—Records of Pioneer Women of Palestine.* New York: Charles L. Brown, 1932.

Maimon, Ada. *Women Build a Land.* Translated by Shulamith Schwarz-Nardi. New York: Herzl Press, 1962.
Yuval, Annabelle. "The Israeli Woman." *Judaism,* Spring
1973, pp. 224–36.

GLOSSARY

agunah a woman who cannot remarry because her husband has deserted her and/or there is no proof that he is dead

aliyah, aliyot being called to recite the Torah blessings or to read from the Torah during a worship service; also, immigration of Jews to Israel

Aliyat HaNoar Hadassah organization founded in 1934 to rescue Jewish children from Europe

Ashkenazic refers specifically to German Jews and their descendants in other countries

ayshet hayil "woman of valor" described in Prov. 31:10-31

baalot keriah women who read from the Torah in the synagogue

Bar/Bat Mitzvah "son/daughter of the commandment"; the mark of a child's growth into young adulthood at the age of thirteen; on reaching Bar/Bat Mitzvah age a boy/girl becomes responsible for his/her own deeds

Beit Din Jewish court of law with a minimum of three members

B'rit Milah the name given the ceremony of circumcision; b'rit means covenant, milah means circumcision

Cohanim members of the priestly class

Ezrat Nashim term for women's section in the Temple; also, name of organization for Jewish women seeking equality within the Jewish community

gaonim   heads of academies of Sura and Pumbedita in Babylonia, sixth to eleventh centuries

get   legal document of divorce

Haboneh   Palestine's largest contracting agency

hakafot   parades around the synagogue in which the Scrolls of the Torah are carried

Halachah   Jewish law; refers particularly to the legal part of Talmudic literature

halitsah   ceremony which releases a man from obligation to marry his brother's widow; necessary only when brother has died without children

hallah   first part of dough set aside for priests; also, loaf of bread used on Shabbat

haluts hana'al   "he that hath his shoe loosed"; recited at conclusion of halitsah ceremony

halutz, halutzah   pioneer

hamantaschen   a three-cornered cake eaten on Purim

Hanukkah   eight day Feast of Lights commemorating victory of Judah Maccabee and followers who defeated the Syrians and rededicated the Temple

Hasidism   religious movement founded by Israel Baal Shem Tov in the eighteenth century in Eastern Europe

heder   elementary Jewish school

Histadrut   Israel's labor federation

hochma   wisdom

huppah   wedding canopy

Kabbalists   those involved in the study and practice of Jewish mysticism

Kaddish   a basic Jewish prayer; in one form, the one most people know, it is the prayer said for the dead

kashrut   the system of laws concerning what a Jew may or may not eat

ketubah   the marriage contract; a paper signed by the bride and the groom, two witnesses, and the rabbi, setting forth the fact of the marriage and its conditions

kibbutz an Israeli communal settlement devoted to agriculture and/or industry

kipah yarmulke, skullcap

Knesset Israeli Parliament

kvutzah, kvutzot a collective agricultural community in Israel smaller than a kibbutz

levir brother-in-law who performs halitsah

l'shana ha-ba'ah b'Yerushalayim "next year in Jerusalem"; hope traditionally expressed at conclusion of Passover seder

mattan voluntary gift given to bride by groom

melamed teacher in an elementary Jewish school

mikvah ritual bath

minyan the quorum of ten necessary for Jewish public worship

mit guten by explanation, reasoning, distraction, and admonishment

mitzvah, mitzvot commandment, a law of God, to do a good or kind deed; to do a mitzvah is to do what God asks of us

Moetzet Hapoalot General Council of Women Workers of Israel founded in 1921 as part of Histadrut

mohar purchase price paid by the groom to the bride's father

moshav Israeli cooperative settlement

nebichdiker Yiddish word referring to an unfortunate person who deserves pity and compassion

nerot candles; refers to a woman's obligation to light Shabbat candles

niddah separation required between husband and wife during wife's menstrual period

nogid leader of a Jewish community; wealthy man

Palmach Israel's self-defense force

Passover festival of freedom commemorating exodus from Egypt

Pidyon HaBen redemption of the firstborn son; a ceremony held on the thirty-first day after birth

Purim holiday based on the Book of Esther celebrating the deliverance of the Jews from Haman's plot to kill them

rebbe religious leader of Hasidic community

rebbetzin rabbi's wife

Rosh Hashanah Jewish New Year

schlemiel Yiddish word meaning dope; person who is good at doing dumb things

schlimazeldiker Yiddish word referring to a person who is unlucky

seder "order"; refers to the ceremony and the meal that is part of the ritual beginning the Passover festival

Sephardic refers to the descendants of those Jews who lived in Spain or Portugal before expulsion in 1492

Shabbat Jewish Sabbath which begins Friday night at sunset and ends Saturday night at sunset

shalom "peace"; Hebrew greeting

Shavuot festival commemorating the giving of the Torah at Mt. Sinai

shelo assani ishah "Who has not made me a woman"; traditional blessing which a man recites each morning

Shema Jewish affirmation of faith; it is biblical in origin

shleehot tzibbur women who lead the congregation in prayer

shtetl small Jewish village in Eastern Europe

shul Yiddish word for synagogue

Simhat Torah the "rejoicing of the Torah," the happy day when the yearlong cycle of reading the Torah ends and the next cycle begins

s'micha ordination; the ceremony of ordaining a rabbi

sotah ordeal described in Num. 5:11-31 which a woman suspected of adultery was forced to undergo

sukkah the hut in which the harvesters lived during the gathering of the fruits at the time of Sukkot, the fall harvest festival

taharat ha-mishpahah family purity

takkanah amendment to the law enacted by halachic scholars

tallit prayershawl

talmid hochem scholar or authority on the Talmud

Talmud commentary on the Bible divided into the Mishnah and the Gemara

tefillin square boxes worn on the forehead and upper arm during morning prayers on weekdays; inside the boxes are parchments containing verses from the Torah

Torah the first of the three parts of the Bible, containing the Five Books of Moses; it is written on a scroll and kept in the Ark in the synagogue

tzitzit fringes on the four corners of the tallit

Ya'al Hadassah's volunteer service organization

yeshivah Talmudic academy

Yom Kippur Day of Atonement; day when Jews seek forgiveness from God and humanity

zelosen pampered, demanding, spoiled

zikah "being chained"; refers to a woman who cannot remarry until her brother-in-law either accepts or refuses levirate marriage

zuzim silver coins worth one-quarter shekel